THOMAS HARDY

THOMAS HARDY

ALBERT J. GUERARD

A NEW DIRECTIONS PAPERBOOK

Library of Congress Catalog Card Number: 64-23651

Published by arrangement with Harvard University Press. For this paperbook reprint the author has added the final section on Hardy's poetry, which has also appeared in *The Sewanee Review*.

ACKNOWLEDGMENT

Quotations from Hardy's poetry by courtesy of The Macmillan Company (New York), publishers of *The Collected Poems of Thomas Hardy*. "The Clasped Skeletons" and "Aristodemus the Messenian" reprinted with permission of The Macmillan Company from *Winter Words* by Thomas Hardy. Copyright 1928 by Florence E. Hardy and Sydney E. Cockerell. Renewed 1956 by Lloyds Bank Ltd. For Canada: Reprinted from *Collected Poems of Thomas Hardy* by permission of The Executors of the Hardy Estate, Macmillan & Co. Ltd., London, and The Macmillan Company of Canada Limited.

Manufactured in the United States of America.

New Directions Books are published by James Laughlin at
Norfolk, Conn. New York office: 333 Sixth Avenue (14)

FOR THE PEARSONS

PREFACE

THIS SMALL BOOK ON THOMAS HARDY was conceived as one of three studies which, taken together, might throw some light on the development of the modern novel, and on the modern novelist's perplexities. The present volume was followed by companion studies: *André Gide* (1951) and *Conrad the Novelist* (1958); this accounts for the frequent appearance of these disturbing names in a book on the kindly and traditional Hardy. They are our points of reference to the darkness that is to come.

My first general intention in examining three such different novelists was to record the impulse away from orthodox realism, classical psychology, and conventional structure; or, the impulse toward the sombre and ironic distortions, the psychological explorations, the dislocations in form of many novelists writing in the middle of the twentieth century. Our three writers clearly represented a progress from one state of art and mind to another; or, perhaps, a decline. Many critics and historians have a vague feeling that "contemporary literature" is an outrage which has been perpetrated while their backs were turned. They wonder what swift and underground process led from Trollope to Kafka and Faulkner; or, even, from the fantasy of Dickens and the probings of Dostoevsky to these. To begin to trace this underground process would require, no doubt, studies of Dickens, Dostoevsky, Faulkner, and Kafka, as well as of Hardy, Conrad, and Gide. But Hardy, Conrad, and Gide are enough to tell us something of what happened to the realistic novel, to our old plausible world, and to ourselves. Hardy does not belong to the old order in the sense that Trollope and George Eliot do. But neither is he a surrealist.

There were further reasons for fixing on this particular triad rather than another. Valuable critical studies have been written on Dickens and Proust and Joyce, for instance, but few satisfactory books on Hardy, Conrad, and Gide as novelists. Many of the studies of Hardy are vitiated by the realistic bias and expectation of post-Victorian critics, or by the academic impulse to confer high seriousness on a writer one likes; some of the studies of Conrad are gossipy contributions by friends; most of the studies of Gide are ethical debates, conducted by scandalized Catholics. Hardy, Conrad, and Gide have long since required revaluation. But if contemporary criticism of fiction as an art seems to be turning fully to Conrad, it has not yet turned sufficiently to Hardy and Gide.

So for our three authors, conceived as roughly representative of the progress of the novel between 1875 and 1925—and conceived as interesting subjects for separate study. Beyond this they have enough in common to make at least casual comparison profitable—surely much more in common than might have been expected, given such radically different attitudes toward the reading public and such differences in that public itself. At the end of the century Conrad, though striving for a large audience, had very few readers and at last expected to be understood only by a saving dozen writers and friends who considered fiction an art. In France at this time André Gide, emerging from the symbolist salons, wrote for a still smaller public and actively discouraged both popularity and comprehension. There was no elite of fiction readers in England, however, when Hardy began to write; had this elite existed, Hardy would probably have ignored it. He too did not really conceive of fiction as a difficult or complex art. He thought of himself as a "purveyor of family fiction" to magazines and wanted to be considered "a good hand at a serial." It was as a poet, not as a novelist, that he hoped and expected to live.

We therefore naturally look in vain, in Hardy, for any technical experiments comparable to Conrad's involutions of time and consciousness or to Gide's novel within a novel within a novel. He offers rather a norm by which the twentieth century's deliberate fragmentations may be measured. Hardy was a dogged, leisurely, old-fashioned storyteller; it was perhaps better so, given the stories he had to tell. But he was a sufficiently conscious artist consciously to rebel against drab and placid realism and in this he anticipates Conrad and Gide. His symbolic use of mischance and coincidence carry us no small distance toward the symbolic use of the absurd in our own time. And the devils or demons shyly suggested in several of Hardy's stories protest, as do Gide's Prometheus and the ambulatory incognito devil of his *Faux-monnayeurs,* against an unimaginative realism and shortsighted science; the ghostly Leggatt and the ghostly James Wait of Conrad make in some respects the same protest. It is perhaps thus, as deliberate anti-realists who yet had realist talents and impulses, that the three novelists seem most closely related—and seem most significant, historically, in the light of contemporary anti-realism. But there are resemblances in matter too, however remote Wessex may seem from Malay and Paris, or from Conrad's Africa and Gide's. Whereas Conrad and Gide are plainly restless exploring psychologists, interested in the major processes of guilt and fear and self-discovery, Hardy may seem merely to dramatize melodramatic oddities of behavior and psychosomatic fantasies. But this is to take a very short view and to fail to read

Hardy's last novels with care. Whatever Hardy intended it to be *The Mayor of Casterbridge,* to take a single example, stands with *Lord Jim* and *L'Immoraliste* among the great dramatic studies of the impulses to self-destruction. Even in personal and moral terms we find much in common in the gentle shy Hardy, the tormented Conrad, and the "satanic" Gide. All three were in some sense lonely men, by skepticism made more lonely, and all three worked beyond mere personal isolation to an understanding of spiritual isolation as the condition of modern man—his condition, ethical destiny, and dilemma. In this respect they revert to a theme which preoccupied the entire nineteenth century. All three further saw the problems raised by collapsing standards and by rapid social change. Hardy, distinctly the least interesting speculative thinker of the three, had contradictory feelings about his tradition-haunted Wessex and sympathized both with those who longed to escape it and those who longed to return. He merely wanted people to be happy. The contradictions of Conrad were far more intense than Hardy's and made him at last (though nihilist, introvert, and destructive explorer of self) the most conservative moralist of his time. His characters are rarely happy and if happy their happiness is irrelevant; Conrad wanted people to be good. Gide, like Hardy, wanted people to be happy, but more than this wanted them to be free. On puritanical grounds he preached happiness and rebellion against convention. It took courage, he insisted, to be free. But the deracinated Lafcadio of Gide is a far advance over the deracinated Clym Yeobright of Hardy, and even over the deracinated Martin Decoud of Conrad; it would be foolish to force them together in the interests of some surface symmetry. Hardy and Conrad seem comparable on many scores, and Conrad and Gide on even more. But Hardy's art and attitude, taken separately, would scarcely seem to promise Gide's, nor Gide's to recall Hardy's.

These are some of the resemblances and differences;

and some of the historical reasons for referring in a book on Hardy to Conrad and Gide. My main interest is nevertheless in Hardy as a novelist rather than in Hardy as a historical presence, and my main purpose is to describe the content and accomplishment of his novels in the simplest possible terms. The present critical study has little to say about Hardy's life and reading or about the London and Dorset of Hardy's day—not merely because much too much has already been said about these things, but also because these things are largely though not wholly irrelevant. I should add at once, frankly, that many of the books on Hardy seem to me vitiated by hardened preconceptions—preconceptions about fatalism and pessimism, for instance—and that the first task of any critic, or of any undergraduate reading Hardy for the first or second time, is to free himself from these preconceptions. It once seemed perverse to have anything to say for *The Return of the Native,* condemned by nearly all reviewers and critics at first; it would now seem perverse to have much to say against it. Yet one must risk seeming perverse in his evaluations and above all in his descriptions. For the first and final task of the critic is to describe what, after proper and prolonged effort, he sees in the work of art; what seems to be as palpably there as the figure in a carpet, and palpably there irrespective of Henry James' figure—irrespective of the declared or supposed intention of the artist. For what is there is the work of art's subject and form; and, incidentally, the product of certain revealed creative impulses (not intentions) which may have been less than conscious, considerably less indeed. The meaning and interest of a novel lie in what the novel says, not in what it was intended to say. And so the critic should be concerned with what the novelist did, not with deciding whether he did what he set out to do.

This study was begun during a year's leave of absence made possible by post-service fellowships granted by the Rockefeller Foundation and the Milton-Clark Fund of

Harvard University. My father and mother, learning that I was embarked on this book, at once read Hardy aloud from cover to cover; and this gave their comments, both of approval and protest, an even greater value than usual. My wife Maclin has once again saved me from many lapses, through her minute care for phrasing and for the state of the manuscript. I am deeply indebted, finally, to Professors Joseph Warren Beach and Harvey Curtis Webster, and to Mrs. Chase Duffy of the Harvard University Press, for their sympathetic and helpful readings of my manuscript.

ALBERT J. GUERARD

Harvard University
December 1, 1948

A volume intended as a general introduction to Hardy cannot, of course, be limited to the novels. I have returned on various occasions to Hardy's poetry, and each time with the feeling that such criticism as I had read did not begin to account for the complex appeals made by Hardy's seemingly simple poems. The re-issue of this volume in the New Directions paperbook series provided a long-awaited challenge and invitation to attempt a first formal assessment of the poetry. This new chapter appeared, in slightly different form, in the Summer, 1964 number of *The Sewanee Review*.

A. J. G.

Stanford-in-France
May 17, 1964

CONTENTS

HARDY AND HIS ADMIRERS

MANY MORE BOOKS ABOUT THOMAS Hardy have already appeared than their subject found time to write himself, and to read them is a long and harrowing task. One rises from this task with the impression that Hardy was a gloomy philosopher (fatalist? mechanistic determinist? meliorist?) who wrote depressing but profound and technically admirable realistic novels. Perhaps the chief motive for still another revaluation is the grossly misleading simplicity of this portrait and, even, its irrelevance. Lascelles Abercrombie was one of Hardy's most penetrating critics, but even he praised the "craftsman" in terms which seem applicable to Flaubert, James, and a very few others, but certainly not to Hardy. To call him a great craftsman is to do injustice both to these complex and conscientious artists and to Hardy himself. For we must begin by recognizing that Hardy was preëminently a traditional teller of tales, and a great poet who stumbled upon the art of fiction and practiced it very waywardly. We must also recognize that his rich and humane imagination accompanied a plodding and at times even commonplace intellect. And we must cling to a first untutored impression that Hardy's novels, read in sequence, are by no means uniformly gloomy. Academic schematizing (the sort of thing which reduces Corneille to the "conflict of will and passion") has done its worst by Hardy. It has fastened on certain obvious structural and didactic aspects of the major Wessex novels to the neglect of much else which remains readable and which can even be useful to a novelist writing today. Whenever a writer shows a certain surface obviousness and a discernible skeleton of intention, commentators may be relied on to gather in great numbers. And this has certainly been true with Hardy, whose art was not that which conceals either art or didactic intention.

There is another reason why Hardy asks for revaluation. Most of Hardy's critics, from Lionel Johnson (1895) to Lord David Cecil (1946), belong to a "generation," and this generation is not ours.* That earlier generation, which I shall call post-Victorian, looked upon its everyday experience as placid, plausible, and reasonably decent; it assumed that the novel should provide an accurate reflection of this sane everyday experience and perhaps a consolation for its rare shortcomings. It assumed that realism was the proper medium of fiction—and that to see a preponderance of evil and brute chance in life was to be unrealistic. In 1871 the *Spectator* thought Hardy absurd for supposing it "possible that an unmarried lady owning an estate could have an illegitimate child";[1] in 1890 Walter Besant asserted that though there are "closed chapters" in the lives of some British men, no British woman "above a certain level" ever commits an indiscretion;[2] in 1938 William Rutland described Arabella and Sue Bridehead as "two such women as are not often found in real life."[3] Does not the same

---

*Needless to say, intellectual generations defy chronology. Joyce and Gide, for instance, belong to a later generation than Samuel Chew, William Rutland, Carl Weber, and Lord David Cecil; that is, Joyce and Gide long ago abandoned attitudes still held by these much younger men.

innocence shine through these three opinions; or, perhaps, the same determination to look on the sweeter side of things?

Much as they liked him, Hardy's post-Victorian critics were made uneasy by his use of melodrama, by his occasional later "nastiness," by his grotesque and macabre deviations from the placid reality they saw. They were drawn to his novels in spite of these things by his exciting Pamela plots and his "Franciscan tenderness in regard to children, animals, laborers, the poor, the mad, the insulted and injured."[4] The gulf between two generations becomes most apparent in the attitude of readers toward this tenderness. To the poet Howard Baker the chief virtue of Hardy's "system" was that "it stiffened and consolidated a mind that otherwise would have been extremely tender and diffuse."[5] Samuel Chew regretted on the other hand that Hardy's novels, though "tender" and "sympathetic," were not "sweet."[6] Mr. Chew's generation, whether it found the sweetness or not, saw Hardy's deliberate anti-realism[7] (his juxtaposition of implausible incident and plausible human character) as a perverse continuation of the Victorian sensation novel. But we now accept Hardy's extreme conjunctions, in the best novels at least, as highly convincing foreshortenings of the actual and absurd world.

We should look on Mr. Chew's generation with envy rather than disrespect, and perhaps we shall have to win our way back to that sweet and gentlemanly confidence. But we have been to a different school. We have rediscovered, to our sorrow, the demonic in human nature as well as in political process; our everyday experience has been both intolerable and improbable, but even more improbable than intolerable. Significantly, Hardy's critics long refused to see that Hardy introduced an at least metaphorical Devil into three of his stories, for the Devil belonged to the improbable middle ages. But today the Devil appears in fiction (from the Devil of Gide to the Devil of Thomas Mann) with increasing frequency, and we can now admit his presence in Hardy. Between the two wars the most vital literary movements, following widely separated paths through reality, arrived at the same conclusions concerning it: that a cosmic absurdity pervades all appearance, that evil has an aggressively real existence, that experience is more often macabre than not. Symbolism, expressionism, and surrealism explored the Freudian labyrinth while naturalism explored the violence latent in society, investigated *bas-fonds* which Zola and Gissing and Bennett never knew. And what both surrealism and naturalism discovered was a more than Gothic horror. This *littérature noire* may give a false picture of our world, but it does help us to suspend disbelief in Hardy's most startling excursions. The famous midnight scene in *Desperate Remedies,* in which Anne Seaway watches Miss Aldclyffe watch a detective watch Manston bury the corpse of his first wife, caused Hardy's genteel and realistically minded critics more distress than any other chapter in his writings. But this extreme foreshortening of reality would seem "probable" enough to the readers of *Les Caves du Vatican, The Castle, The Wild Goose Chase, Au Château d'Argol*—and *Intruder in the Dust.* William Faulkner has consistently used the distortions of popular storytelling—exaggeration, grotesque horror, macabre coincidence—to achieve his darker truth; they are part of his reading of life. Just so Hardy made something visionary out of Victorian coincidence by juxtaposing the fantastic and the everyday.

There are several reasons for the increasing sensationalism of serious modern fiction. Perhaps the most alarming one is that we are victims of a law of diminishing returns. We are preoccupied with defining guilt and evil, but the disappearance of social convention makes a definition of evil through behavior exceedingly difficult. The fictional heroine or villainess who in 1870 permitted a premarital kiss must in 1915 commit adultery if she wishes to provoke the same horror in her readers; by 1945 she must be a pervert or a murderess. (Similarly, an Anne Seaway can no longer dispose of and hide a poisoned drink by pouring it into the bosom of her dress, an Elfride can no longer summon enough underclothing to fashion a lifesaving rope, and a Captain De Stancy is no longer likely to be inflamed by the spectacle of a young lady in a pink flannel gymnasium suit.) The modern novelist is often more concerned with the problem of good and evil than his Victorian predecessor was, though less concerned with the problem of social conformity. But he no longer has at hand accepted symbols with which to dramatize that problem conveniently. And he must convince a reader who has seen a good deal of horror himself. A great artist—but only a great artist, an Elizabeth Bowen, for instance—can still create a quiet fictional world and provoke the reader's moral judgment by showing minute deviations from that quiet norm. Hardy limited himself in this fashion once, in *Under The Greenwood Tree,* with notable success. This deliberately slight early work is not Hardy's greatest novel, but it strikes me as his most perfect work of art.

More legitimately, the contemporary novelist wants to express a vision of the world rather than to give an accurate picture of Main Street or the Five Towns. Even the naturalistic novel is in full reaction against a realism which reduced art to photography and which bored two generations of readers. If the more respectable of the best sellers are still in bondage to the hard stubborn facts and massive probabilities of Galsworthy and Bennett, the best contemporary novelists are trying to recover Stendhal's daring economy, Melville's freedom to indulge fantasy and speculation, Dickens' sheer and abundant creativity. When the sombre metaphysical interpreters have had their say, we may come to admire Kafka and Faulkner above all for their great inventiveness and Graham Greene for his ability to tell a story. And we are now willing to go back to Hardy for the qualities which in 1920 seemed so old-fashioned: the absurd coincidences, the grotesque heightenings of reality, the sense of mystery inhabiting hostile circumstance and nature itself. We go back too for the tales themselves—as stark and tragic and traditional as any ballads.[8] We are no longer willing to dismiss some of Hardy's finest inventions, as does Mr. Chew—Sergeant Troy's sword exercise, Henchard's sale of his wife, Knight suspended on the face of the cliff, the gambling on the heath in *The Return of the Native,* the death of Jude's children—merely because they are "sensational" and "too remote from ordinary experience." We are in fact attracted by much that made the post-Victorian realist uneasy: the inventiveness and improbability, the symbolic use of reappearance and coincidence, the wanderings of a macabre imagination, the suggestions of supernatural agency; the frank acknowledgement that love is basically sexual and marriage usually unhappy; the demons of plot, irony, and myth. And we are repelled or left indifferent by what charmed that earlier generation: the regionalist's ear for dialect, the botanist's eye for the minutiae of field and tree, the architect's eye for ancient mansions, and the farmer's eye for sheepshearings; the pretentious meditation on Egdon Heath;[9] the discernible architecture of the novels and the paraphrasable metaphysic; the Franciscan tenderness and sympathy—and, I'm afraid, the finally unqualified faith in the goodness of a humanity more sinned against than sinning. We can say this without re-creating Hardy in the image of our own difficulties and intentions. Hardy was in many ways a Victorian and may well have been, as Lord David Cecil says, the last of the Elizabethans.[10] I merely mean that we are less likely to be disturbed by Hardy's Victorian or Elizabethan oddities than was the reader of Arnold Bennett; and, possibly, we are more willing to be entertained.

Perhaps the commonest fault of academic criticism is its tendency to reduce the aesthetic reality to simple and plausible formulae: most obviously, to reduce a poem's meaning to the sum of its paraphrasable statements or a novel's meaning to some philosophy of life. It is only too easy to theorize oneself quite away from the living complex of the work of art and the impression it actually makes. A basic fact about Hardy's novels is that they are very hard to put down; some primary energy and suspense carries the reader through the clumsiest and most pedantic chapters. Another basic fact is that Hardy had a very strong sense of fun. The impulse to comedy is likely to appear at highly inopportune moments. In *A Pair of Blue Eyes* Hardy finds it hard to decide whether Elfride's funeral train—with two suitors on board, ignorant of her marriage and death, and for a while ignorant of each other—should be considered more ludicrous than tragic or more tragic than ludicrous. But Hardy's qualities as a popular entertainer and writer of comedy have been submerged under a great deal of sombre theorizing about his philosophy; Hardy the thinker has overwhelmed Hardy the teller of tales. It is certainly true that Hardy had a vision of the cosmic absurd—of man's longing for order and justice outraged by the eternal indifferent drift of things[11]—and his attitude toward this conception of the human dilemma is one of the shaping forces of his work. But it is much less rewarding to dwell on his iteration of some of the intellectual conclusions of his time: whether those of John Stuart Mill or Comte or von Hartmann or Bergson. As a thinker Hardy is commonplace in juxtaposition to Bergson; he is commonplace even in juxtaposition to Comte. A poet's ideas on society or on the cosmos are no subtler nor more rewarding because they happen to be a poet's. Yet academic critics often applaud poetic speculation whose crudity they would never tolerate from a colleague.

The Dynasts has of course suffered most of all from these didactic interpretations; it has been treated, in spite of Hardy's forewarnings and protests, as a philosophical essay, rather than as a historical and dramatic poem. The observing Spirits (originally conceived as a technical means of transcending threadbare analytic realism in the novel)[12] have now quite superseded the drama they observe; the Spirit of the Years has even been equated with the Freudian ego and the Spirit of the Pities with the superego.[13] The untutored reader must surely find *The Dynasts* an uneven but absorbing chronicle of historical events and persons: Napoleon and Pitt and Alexander are alive and interesting in spite of Hardy's theoretical determinism, just as Zola's characters are alive and interesting in spite of his theoretical determinism. And surely the Spirits, once they have helped us to a daring point of view, are little more than embodied attitudes. A familiar chain of reasoning can prove, however, that determined characters are not, properly speaking, characters at all, and it is this implacable logic which leads W. R. Rutland to conclude that the Spirits "are the only real characters in the *Dynasts*"![14] Flawless reasoning, as it appears, has led an intelligent reader as far away as possible from an unprejudiced reading of the poem, from the impression the poem actually makes, from what it really says. Nearly all discussions of Hardy's thought fail to distinguish between formulated belief and dramatically useful symbol or myth.

Worse still, even the simplest of the novels have been reread as adumbrations of *The Dynasts* and its grotesque philosophizing. Most of Hardy's critics have observed his talent for dramatizing feminine capriciousness. From Cytherea and Elfride and Fancy Day to Sue Bridehead and the three Avice Caros his charming unregenerate heroines have a hard time making up their minds and change them as soon as they have made them up. Hardy looked on these women with fascination, love, and bitterness, and I suspect he had more of an artist's pleasure with them than with his more massive creations. But even these amusing heroines fall under *The Dynasts*' shadow: "What in these women seems a lack of volition is due to their being possessed by the Will."[15] The far more fleshly Arabella (it would be hard to conceive of a less abstract characterization) is for Mr. Hedgcock "le vouloir-vivre incarné et inconscient"[16] and for Mr. Chew "the tool of the Will-to-Live."[17] In fairness to Hardy's critics we should acknowledge at once that the novelist, himself much given to schematizing, often led his readers astray both in his prefaces and in his occasional didactic asides. The unprepared reader is likely to find the first twelve chapters of *Two on a Tower,* for instance, a high comedy in the French manner and the rest a contrived drama of cross-purposes, ill luck, and the slow death of love. But what critic could resist (or has resisted) the first neat sentence of Hardy's misleading preface? "This slightly built romance was the outcome of a wish to set the emotional history of two infinitesimal lives against the stupendous background of the stellar universe, and to impart to readers the sentiment that of these contrasting magnitudes the smaller might be the greater to them as men." On some occasions Hardy's dramatic energy was sufficient for the novels to survive their schematic intentions; on other occasions it was not. In *Two on a Tower,* at least, Hardy became much more interested in the wholly human conflict between simplicity and complexity of temperament than in his announced subject.

I do not wish to protest against the presence of reasoning in criticism. But reasoning on art can very easily escape the art it reasons on and construct syllogisms which are logically perfect but pragmatically absurd. This evasion of the aesthetic reality may occur even in reasoning on description and style. Thus Lord David Cecil, analyzing the first paragraph of the second chapter of *The Return of the Native:* *

---

* "Along the road walked an old man. He was white-headed as a mountain, bowed in the shoulders, and faded in general aspect. He wore a glazed hat, an ancient boat-cloak, and shoes; his brass buttons bearing an anchor upon their face. In his hand was a silver-headed walking-stick, which he used as a veritable third leg, perseveringly dotting the ground with its point at every few inches' interval. One would have said that he had been, in his day, a naval officer of some sort or other."

> The broad features are firmly set before us—the road and the old man. We see him in scale and proportion to the landscape, which is his setting. This is in the large, heroic, descriptive manner of Scott. But Hardy does not stop when he has given us the broad outline, as Scott does. Here he is more like Richardson. He goes into every detail—the old man's hat, his buttons and his characteristic sailor's gait—*so that there are no vague, vacant intervals in the picture which may blur our full impression.* The scene is complete.[18]

The premise is that the receptive imagination is a canvas on which a painting may be composed and on which every brushstroke remains fresh and in place; given this premise, Lord David's reasoning is flawless. But the premise is of course false, the more so because readers refuse to advance at two pages an hour. It is virtually impossible to convey an exact visual scene from one mind to another through the medium of words, as eighteenth-century rhetoricians well remembered but many Victorian novelists forgot. What the novelist can do is to offer a few sharp invigorating details—details which will rouse the reader's sluggish image-making powers—and then hope these awakened shaping powers will fashion some sufficiently appropriate image. It is precisely the "vacant intervals" which allow the reader freedom to move around and make his own picture. Hardy's description of the old man is striking enough, but it operates by suggestion rather than photography; I doubt that many readers visualize the anchors on the brass buttons, but those who do are in danger of losing everything else. Since a reader is active, if he is a reader at all, his visualization can only be blurred by the accumulation of minute details, by "completeness." I open *The Red and the Black* and find this:

> This Duke was a man of fifty, dressed like a dandy, and *treading as though on springs.* He had a narrow head with a large nose, and a *curved face which he kept thrusting forward.* It would have been hard for anyone to appear at once so noble and so insignificant.

The last sentence perhaps goes beyond a debatable limit of vagueness for the sake of momentary wit. And there are many "vacant intervals." But the italicized words offer major invigorating details which for one reader at least create a visible presence (though not, I suppose, the presence Stendhal saw). Hardy has been justly and repeatedly praised for his preparation for the great storm in *Far from the Madding Crowd,* for his ability to convey a sense of changing oppression and terror. But this impression is achieved either through striking metaphor ("A light *flapped* over the scene") or, more commonly, through a frank and extended use of macabre suggestion; and even, as in the italicized phrases, through a daring appeal to recollections of childhood terror:

> He put out the expiring lights, that the barn might not be endangered, closed the door upon the men in their deep and oblivious sleep, and went again into *the lone night.* A hot breeze, as if breathed from the *parted lips of some dragon about to swallow the globe,* fanned him from the south, while directly opposite in the north rose a *grim misshapen* body of cloud, in the very teeth of the wind. So unnaturally did it rise that one could fancy it to be lifted by *machinery from below.* Meanwhile the faint *cloudlets* had flown back into the southeast corner of the sky, *as if in terror of the large cloud, like a young brood gazed in upon by some monster.*[19]

There is no question here of auditory or visual exactness, or of "completeness."

My argument is that Hardy's post-Victorian critics, confronted by their own very strong affection for his books, have tried to find academic, formal, respectable reasons for this feeling; they have tried to discover not merely a philosopher and a realist but a minute and subtle craftsman. They have looked for serious purpose behind the most wayward and spontaneous. It is hard to understand, otherwise, why they should have singled out for praise what today seems one of Hardy's gravest weaknesses: his tendency to shape and plan his novels according to some obvious architectual principle and his failure to conceal the blueprint. The crucial problem (and cardinal virtue) of form in the novel is one which can be debated endlessly. It distributes itself into such particular technical questions as the distance from which the author views his characters and the distance from which he views his readers; the casualness with which he manages transitions in time and emphasis; the control which he exerts over his own energy; the ruthlessness with which he suppresses the charming and irrelevant; the coherence with which he establishes and maintains an attitude; the courage with which he transcends mere liquidation of his feelings while continuing to exploit them; the economy and unerring accuracy, in brief, of his by no means obvious art. All this is indeed endlessly debatable, but at least it would seem axiomatic (for Hardy's kind of fiction) that the blueprint should never appear; that the novelist's skeletal outline and timetables should be wholly submerged in the finished product; that art should conceal art.

Perhaps because of his architectural training, Hardy did think of "beauty of shape" in fiction in external and diagrammatic terms; he had little to say, in his three brief critical essays, about these subtler aspects of form.[20] Here again not a few of his critics have followed him docilely. Lionel Johnson set the tone, perhaps, when he found "evidence in plenty" that Hardy's work was "full of conscious pains."[21] Now, at a distance of half a century, it would be hard to conceive of fainter praise. Even Lascelles Abercrombie, surprisingly enough, described the rigid counterpoint grouping of *Far from the Madding Crowd, The Return of the Native,* and *The Woodlanders* as "three expressions of formal mastery," and reduced the "concatenated affections" in these books to neat algebraic formulae.[22] *The Return of the Native,* whose main action covers exactly a year and a day, and which was conceived in terms of physics rather than of algebra,[23] has given particular pleasure to those who like to discern an author's skeletal outline. Joseph Warren Beach, who later wrote exceedingly penetrating criticism of fiction, once praised the *Return's* "logical massing" of its material and its adherence to the unities of place and time. Conversely, he complained because *The Woodlanders* was not divided into parts, because the chapters were given no titles, and because the transitions in time and place were managed casually rather than formally.[24]

Such formalism might be harmless, if it did not interfere with judgment on more complex matters and were it not for the fact that Hardy's fiction in general and *The Return of the Native* in particular are annually presented to American students as touchstones of the art of fiction. It is more disturbing to find that both Mr. Beach and Mr. Chew dismiss *Under the Greenwood Tree* very casually. However slight in subject, and in spite of the fact that the first center of interest (the Mellstock Choir) surrenders to the second (the little romance) rather than blends with it, the book is certainly one of Hardy's finest structural achievements. As different as possible in tone, *The Mayor of Casterbridge* is Hardy's other stylized masterpiece—a simply conceived and ancient tragedy whose formality (the fateful return of the furmity-woman, the return to the fairground, etc.) seems justified by the grandeur and simplicity of its myth. Mr. Beach regards *The Mayor of Casterbridge* as even farther than *The Woodlanders* "from the method of sober and shapely drama."[25] But *Under the Greenwood Tree,* that "rural painting of the Dutch School," is as formal as a miniature, and *The Mayor of Casterbridge* (though too long) is as formal as a block of stone.[26]

These then are some of the obstacles which criticism has placed between the reader and the novels themselves. Criticism has refused, in its devotion to realism, to recognize the strength and validity of Hardy's anti-realistic aim and has often deplored his imaginative heightenings of reality; it has subordinated the simple and traditional storyteller to the gloomy philosopher of the Will; it has ignored a very large vein of comedy while allowing the existence of rustic humor; it has lavished praise on Hardy's superficial architectonics, while passing over the subtle beauty of his few formal triumphs. The conventional view of Hardy as normally gloomy depends in large part on the relative critical neglect of the "minor" novels. Hardy's achievement has long since been reduced to six or at most seven novels, and it is fashionable to praise nearly everything in these particular books and to condemn very nearly everything in the others. Even if this conventional division into major and minor novels were absolutely satisfactory, and it is relatively satisfactory, the minor novels would be worth closer attention. For the failures of a great writer can often teach us as much as his triumphs, and this is particularly true where, as in *Two on a Tower* and *A Laodicean,* the failures begin brilliantly. It would be possible to use even *The Hand of Ethelberta* as a textbook in the art of fiction, so easy is it to point to the places where creative energy operates, flags, then fitfully reappears.

There is of course nothing more demoralizing than the indiscriminate approval of everything which happens to appear in an acknowledged masterpiece. To say that Hardy's descriptions "are never detachable ornament" or that his reference to painters are not a "mere parade of knowledge"[27] is to justify intrinsic and indefensible lapses. Lionel Johnson's assumption that Hardy never mutilated his books in deference to public prejudice[28] should serve as an eternal warning to critics that even great writers are human. Finally, most of Hardy's critics have observed that his women are more successful creations than his men, but few of them have pointed out the exceptional inadequacy of these men both as fictional characters and as human beings. Henchard and Jude are astounding exceptions to one of the most conspicuous "vacant places" in the composition of any major writer. To explain this failing adequately may require psychological data which are not yet available. But the failure must be frankly recognized. To describe Boldwood and Alec D'Urberville as successful characterizations[29] (merely because they happen to appear in superior books?) is to demoralize judgment. Hardy can certainly survive our frankest recognitions.[30]

The didactic impulse in Hardy is too strong to be ignored, but we may touch upon it slightly as standing on the fringe of his achievement. The thought of a novelist does matter, where the thinking mind is an André Gide's or a Thomas Mann's or even an Aldous Huxley's. Joseph Conrad gives the impression of a haunted and distinguished mind in his most reactionary as in his most nihilistic hours; this intellectual distinction leaves its mark on his best novels, down to the slightest turn of phrase. Hardy's mind, on the other hand, was haunted but intellectually unsubtle; the commonplaceness betrays itself in a certain doggedness of reasoning and in the fewness and banality of his characters' dilemmas. At the poetic and imaginative level, where he dramatizes human feelings rather than thinks about subjects, Hardy's mind was anything but commonplace; it was capable of tragedy. But it would be very rash to look on most of his novels as serious spiritual histories of an age, in the sense that Arnold's poems are spiritual histories of an age. Even Hardy's greatest intellectual problem, how to reconcile the scientific and the spiritual attitudes toward life,[31] scarcely appears, as such, in the novels—though it appears repeatedly in the poems and in the choruses of *The Dynasts.* If we except *Jude the Obscure,* Hardy was much less concerned with immediate problems than Gissing, and even much less than Wilkie Collins. Here as elsewhere Hardy, who read little contemporary fiction, escaped the overwhelming influence of Dickens. He was most truly the spiritual historian of the age in his temperamental rather than in his formal pessimism; in his pictures of lonely men standing shyly outside the active current of life rather than in his explicit rejections.

He did not, that is, keep a careful finger on the changing pulse of the age; very few English novelists did so. Is there any English counterpart to Paul Bourget, whose novels dramatize successively the changing intellectual convictions of half a century: Taine's determinism, the reaction against determinism, the psycho-physiology of Janet, the dangers of modern introspection and of cosmopolitanism and of class-deracination, the return to Catholicism, the fallacies of modernism in religion, the value of psychiatry, the value of William James's pragmatism, the dangers of psychiatry and pragmatism, the decadence of France on the eve of the great war, the excesses of the post-war decade?[32] Bourget, who began by writing what are still among the best studies of intellectual history in the nineteenth century *(Essais de psychologie contemporaine),* so exhausted all possible "subjects" that he finally wrote a novel on the problems of boy scouts. Bourget was actually an exceptionally intelligent man. By trying to keep abreast of changing opinion, however, he repeatedly found himself left behind. He is worth mentioning here as a startling answer to the dictum that a novelist should reflect his age explicitly. His ruthless and often intelligent contemporaneity makes him largely unreadable now.

Unlike Gide, Hardy is least interesting where he is most theoretical; he begins to plot his situations and characters abstractly only when dramatic energy fails. *(Jude the Obscure* is again an exception, since the source of the didacticism is less cool reasoning than an energizing indignation.) But Hardy was first of all a storyteller, and his attitude toward many problems was aesthetic. His pessimism was genuine enough, of course, but it was to a degree cultivated as artistically useful. He knew that if some natures become vocal in comedy, his own became vocal in tragedy.[33] In 1877 he resolved to make nature's defects "the basis of a hitherto unperceived beauty" because in doing so he could transcend "mechanical reporting."[34] His New Year's thought for 1879 is on the aesthetic usefulness rather than the scientific validity of fatalism: "A perception of the FAILURE of THINGS to be what they are meant to be, lends them, in place of the intended interest, a new and greater interest of an unintended kind."[35] Fatalism was a dramatically useful myth, as any reader of the popular ballads could see. And so too was the myth of the Will. Every student of *The Dynasts* should recall that the "system" had its origin in the desire to transcend analytic realism in the novel through symbolism.[36]

We are thus confronted by a writer who, however sincere his convictions, thought first of all of his stories. Even the historian of Wessex knew that Wessex was dramatically useful, thanks to the presence of elementary passions in a circumscribed world, thanks to "the concentrated passions and closely knit interdependence of the lives therein."[37] But should we accept the novels as a historical record of changes in Dorset from 1800 to 1889? One of Hardy's great "subjects" was, of course, the sad passing of the stable rural life, the decay of old customs and of local traditions, the death of ghost stories and the death of village choirs. The agricultural laborers in *Under the Greenwood Tree,* laid in about 1835,[38] belong to that stable and cheerful old England; they are at most threatened by the modern manners of a Fancy Day and by her anachronistic player-organ. By 1869-1873, however, the time of *Far from the Madding Crowd,* the laborer is already less secure; the hiring-fair is a sinister annual event, the migration of labor has begun. In *Tess of the D'Urbervilles* (1884-1889), Old Lady Day is a tragic time; the roads are choked with the pitiful carts of the migrating farm laborers and the dispossessed artisan cottagers. Only the Talbothays dairy remains as a green oasis in a Wessex which has become sombre and bleak. We are left with the unmistakable impression that the farm laborer has lost not only his ancient memories and folk customs but also the reasonable comforts of life.

The historical fact was quite different, as Hardy acknowledged to Rider Haggard in 1902:

> As to your first question, my opinion on the past of the agricultural labourers in this county: I think, indeed know, that down to 1850 or 1855 their condition was in general one of great hardship. I say in general, for there have always been fancy-farms, resembling St. Clair's in *Uncle Tom's Cabin*. . . To go to the other extreme: as a child I knew a sheep-keeping boy who to my horror shortly afterwards died of want—the contents of his stomach at the autopsy being raw turnip only. . . Between these examples came the great bulk of farms. . .
>
> Secondly: as to the present. Things are of course widely different now. I am told that at the annual hiring-fair just past, the old positions were absolutely reversed, the farmers walking about and importuning the labourers to come and be hired. . . Their present life is almost without exception one of comfort, if the most ordinary thrift be observed. I could take you to the cottage of a shepherd not many miles from here that has a carpet and brass-rods to the staircase, and from the open door of which you hear a piano strumming within. . .
>
> But changes at which we must all rejoice have brought other changes which are not so attractive. The labourers have become more and more migratory—the younger families in especial. . . The consequences are curious and unexpected. For one thing, village tradition—a vast mass of unwritten folk-lore, local chronicle, local topography, and nomenclature—is absolutely sinking, has nearly sunk, into eternal oblivion. . . Thus you see, there being no continuity of environment in their lives, there is no continuity of information, the names, stories, and relics of one place being speedily forgotten under the incoming facts of the next.[39]

There are no starving shepherds in *Under the Greenwood Tree* and *Far from the Madding Crowd;* there is very little prosy suffering. We may explain this, of course, by Hardy's increasing pessimism between 1872 and 1891, when part of *Tess* was serialized. But we would still have to acknowledge that the decay of old customs was more significant to Hardy the novelist than the amelioration of the laborer's lot; the aesthetic changes were the ones which concerned him. The dialogue of his rustics was no more realistic than that of Shakespeare's rustics; their daily security and moral innocence were, perhaps, very nearly as idealized. Hardy was not the historian of Dorset but the novelist and poet of Wessex. He was a realist within a world he had reshaped to his vision and whose joys and sorrows he had quite deliberately heightened. "Alas, the peasants have almost died out," Hardy complained to Arthur Symons in 1926.[40] It was the novelist who spoke, rather than the free citizen of Dorchester.

Hardy thus looked on the problems of Dorset and Wessex as raw material for his vision and drama; he distorted actuality to achieve a kind of truth which Bourget never knew. A few very real though somewhat rudimentary problems recur in most of the novels and provide a formal subject matter: the contrast between rural simplicity and urban or aristocratic complexity and corruption, the pathos of regional and class deracination, the destructive effect of class feeling, the problem of marriage and mismarriage, and the conflicting impulses toward spontaneity and tradition or convention. Only in *Tess* and *Jude* does Hardy face the characteristic nightmares of the late Victorian age: the problem of ethics without dogma and the problem of the restless and isolated modern ego. *The Mayor of Casterbridge,* though it anticipates modern speculations on the self-destructive impulse, retains a massive antiquity. But in *Jude the Obscure* we recognize our own world; we even recognize some of our friends.

Hardy appears to have taken his extreme contrast between Wessex and London fairly seriously. When his own transported servants flirted shamelessly with the London delivery boys (much as did those in *The Hand of Ethelberta*) he was alarmed. But he also took this to be proof of their naïve rustic innocence.[41] He acknowledged that there was coarseness in rural life, but not "that libidinousness which makes the scum of cities so noxious."[42] Vice exists, but on the far lurid horizon of Budmouth Regis (miles beyond Egdon and Froom Vale) or even farther away in Bath. Women may be led astray at dances and fairs, of course, or be seduced by itinerant soldiers; such is the way of the world. The Mixen Lane of Casterbridge is Hardy's only hint of a permanent underworld. Even there —where peasants met "who combined a little poaching with their farming, and a little brawling and bibbing with their poaching"—vice is amiable and rural, and prostitution can be passed off in a single apologetic sentence. The eternal drama of love and its unforeseen consequences is accepted by the rustics themselves as casually and tolerantly as the seasons, and often as humorously too. No more calculation enters into it than enters into the seasons; all the Hardy rustics are innocents, and most of them are healthily free from remorse. This too will go onward the same, this acceptance of what life has to offer, though dynasties pass. Hardy nowhere idealizes his rustics more successfully than in showing the kindness of Tess's fellow workers as she nurses her child in the field; we accept the idealization even after we have read Hardy's admission that the lot of the girl with an illegitimate child is much easier in crowded cities.[43] The great Wessex virtues are fidelity, simplicity, endurance, and tolerance.

This rural simplicity, the equilibrium of unreflective acceptance, is threatened by aristocratic or urban complexity, by invaders from the outside world. It is scarcely an accident that Lucetta Le Sueur and the one-time actress Felice Charmond (with her "adaptable, wandering *weltburgerliche* nature") should have French names, or that some of the masculine invaders— Aeneas Manston, William Dare, Dr. Fitzpiers, and the Baron von Xanten for instance—should seem ambassadors from a still more infernal country.[44] These intruders (to put aside for the moment the question of diabolic origins) corrupt the Wessex innocents by their flashy city manners: Sergeant Troy adds the taint of aristocratic blood to his military irresponsibility and glamor. "The Fiddler of the Reels," one of the finest short stories in the language, excellently illustrates Hardy's formula. The fiddler Wat or "Mop" Ollamoor, very un-English in appearance, comes to Stickleford "from nobody knew where." The "chromatic subtleties" of his violin give him a weird and wizardly power over unsophisticated rural maidens. He plays on their simple feelings until they become hysterical and then seduces them. Car'line Aspent, in whom hysteria reaches epileptic proportions, repudiates Ned Hipcroft, her village lover; the disillusioned Ned goes off to London and eventually becomes a mechanic at the great Hyde Park Exhibition of 1851. Four years pass and Car'line delicately suggests to Ned by letter that she had made a mistake in refusing him. Ned, simple rustic that he is, agrees to forgive her; he even accepts, after only a few minutes' hesitation, the wholly unexpected presence of Mop Ollamoor's child. A year after Car'line has joined Ned the two Wessex refugees long for the simplicities of home. On their way back to Stickleford they are separated briefly, and at a country inn Car'line hears again Mop's violin. She cannot resist joining the dance; more and more hysterical, she dances on after all the others have stopped and finally she falls to the floor in convulsions. When she comes to herself, both Mop and the child are gone. They are never found, though it is rumored that the fiddler made the child dance on stilts at a London fair, and at last took her to America. We now recall that Car'line had caught a momentary disturbing glimpse of Mop at the Hyde Park Exhibition. For the Exhibition stands behind the story as a symbol of the collision between two ways of life—the simple old country life and the complex, disturbing, and urban new.[45]

The fascinators with their mesmeric powers are sometimes also endowed with the "Mephistophelian element, brains": William Dare, the extreme example of diabolic cosmopolitanism, could be described as a walking intellect, while Dr. Fitzpiers' casual seductions must certainly be related to his reading of philosophical treatises. George Somerset in *A Laodicean* has a kind of rural patience, but Clym Yeobright is Hardy's only idealized intellectual—idealized because he returns to his native heath and achieves a Tolstoian simplicity there. The urban or aristocratic hedonists form another group of intruders on rustic simplicity: the Alec D'Urbervilles, the Felice Charmonds, the Charles Rayes. (Significantly, Raye is "full of vague latter-day glooms and popular melancholies.")[46] These persons, who have abandoned dogma, also have too much time on their hands for their own good and for the good of hard-working folk. But it is important to recall that the overfastidious prudes transgress on Wessex simplicity as harmfully as the deliberate or casual seducers. The insufferable Angel Clare contaminates the green innocence of Talbothays. And in "For Conscience' Sake" Millborne ruins the life of a woman he had seduced many years before by compelling her to make him an honest man. Here at least, in this story of 1891, Hardy regarded fastidiousness in ethics and feeling as signs "of the century's decadence."

The collision of simple and complex temperament provokes some of *Two on a Tower's* tragedy, but the differences are not primarily regional. The contrast and collision, regarded frankly as regional, is of course the explicit subject of *The Woodlanders.* The novel opens brilliantly with an extreme violation of natural right and property: Felice Charmond's purchase of Marty South's hair. Mrs. Charmond has come to the snug little world of the Hintocks, bringing with her the sophisticated ennui and consequent sentimentality of the overcivilized world outside. Dr. Fitzpiers brings not only a disturbing fondness for philosophy, but also temperamental complexity: "the fineness of tissue which could take a deep, emotional—almost an artistic—pleasure in being the yearning *inamorato* of a woman he had once deserted."* And even Grace Melbury,

*It is worth noting that the isolation of the Hintocks palls on Dr. Fitz-

who has been away to a fashionable school, returns unable to tell one apple tree from another and with a restless longing for luxury and trips to Europe. Giles Winterborne and Marty South are the tragic victims of this invading complexity, but the moral is pointed more subtly in Mr. Melbury's loss of ancient and necessary certitudes. Nowhere does Hardy so clearly anticipate the Conrad of *The Nigger of the Narcissus* and *Typhoon,* who idealized extrovert simplicity:

> He had entirely lost faith in his own judgment. That judgment on which he had relied for so many years seemed recently, like a false companion unmasked, to have disclosed unexpected depths of hypocrisy and speciousness where all had seemed solidity. He felt almost afraid to form a conjecture on the weather, or the time, or the fruit-promise, so great was his self-abasement.[47]

Criticism has perhaps exaggerated the flatness of Hardy's portraits of fashionable life; Neigh and Mountclere are convincing enough. (He goes farthest astray, curiously enough, when his sophisticates discuss literature.)[48] But as a novelist at least Hardy was willing to agree with the repentant Grace: "honesty, goodness, manliness, tenderness, devotion, for her only existed in their purity now in the breasts of unvarnished men."

Grace Melbury is deracinated from class as well as from region, and she makes her strongest claim on our sympathy when she longs once more for the old primitive life. So too does the heroine of "The Son's Veto," Sophy Twycott, who marries the parson she had once served as parlor maid, instead of Sam Hobson, and who must leave her friendly North Wessex village for an idle and lonely life in London. Years later she loses the faithful Sam for a second time, when her snobbish son down from Oxford makes her kneel and swear not to marry beneath her. The pathos of her deracination is underlined by the pleasure she takes

---

piers because he has no local memories, and cannot enjoy the sustaining companionship of "old association."

in a clandestine wagon ride to the Covent Garden market, perched on a mass of cabbages. Hardy sympathizes with the love that knows not class barriers, and with the native's aspirations for a richer intellectual life. But the way of deracination is sorrow. In *Two on a Tower* Swithin St. Cleeve, son of a curate and a farmer's daughter, grows up in a community which has no definite social status to offer such an anomaly as he; in *A Pair of Blue Eyes* Stephen Smith, who has become an architect's assistant, is uncomfortable both at the parsonage and among his parents' friends. And Jude Fawley—uprooted from his home, his class, and even his religious faith—is Henchard's only rival in the suffering induced by moral isolation. The native must return to his homeland and roots for peace of mind, where he may enjoy the companionship of "old association." In 1883, Hardy himself returned to Dorchester, to build his house and live.

Hardy dramatizes the evil of class feeling—how "honest human affection will become shamefaced and mean under the frost of class-division and social prejudices"[49]—in nearly all his stories and novels. An interesting sentence in *An Indiscretion in the Life of an Heiress* suggests that the love which transcends class barriers, however difficult for the lover, can ease the novelist's task in an unexpected way.[50] But Hardy's preoccupation with the theme was sincere enough and even almost obsessive—whether we trace it to the child's devotion to the *grande dame* of his native parish or to the first Mrs. Hardy's lifelong social aspirations and unshakable conviction that she (the niece of an Archdeacon of London) had certainly married beneath her. The ambition to rise above one's class can leave little time for love; it can even be so strong as to lead to crime, as in the short story "A Tragedy of Two Ambitions." More often Hardy presents class feeling as the conventional obstacle to true love and as the final destroyer of love not so true. When Thomasin sees the scrubbed and whitened Diggory she discovers that beauty is more than skin deep. This is literary convention reduced almost to self-satire, and we are relieved to know that Hardy had planned no such happy ending. But on at least three occasions Hardy treated the class problem other than conventionally.

In *The Hand of Ethelberta* the heroine, at first a lifeless caricature of the intellectual female, suddenly acquires some of Bathsheba Everdene's indomitable courage; her will to make a good marriage is in fact the will to hold her family together, the proletarian will to survive. But in the midst of her campaign, which is as unselfish as it is ruthless, she feels the anxiety of class guilt; she is almost the only character in Hardy to do so.[51] Like *The Hand of Ethelberta, A Laodicean* is generally regarded a complete failure. The novel does indeed collapse after the first one hundred and forty pages, but the opening chapters are among the finest and most controlled Hardy ever wrote. Somerset's introduction into the Power household, his bored curiosity, and his willingness to compromise his architectural principles for the lovely Paula's sake are presented with some of the subtlety of Gide's *Isabelle.* And Paula's own feeling for the castle and the De Stancys—the longing of the new moneyed aristocracy to ally itself with the old aristocracy of blood—would of course have been a tempting subject for Edith Wharton and Henry James. All this is introduced in a tone of cool high comedy. But as the book proceeds the problem of class feeling becomes a mere conventional obstacle and device of plot, and the charmingly modern and ambiguous Paula degenerates into a paragon of Victorian smugness and evasion.*

---

*The Victorian heroine is of course a late descendant of courtly love. She dictatorially "permits" men to accompany her and draws a fine line as to exactly what they may or may not say about anything. If medieval courtly love was a saving veneer which concealed wholesale adultery (adultery which for various social reasons was "necessary"), we are tempted to look on the attitude toward women in Victorian popular fiction as chivalric idealization which had no saving fleshly grace or excuse. Paula is a good example.

In *The Hand of Ethelberta* and *A Laodicean* Hardy saw the problem of class feeling in other than conventional terms, but lacked the dramatic energy and control to vivify his fresh insight. But in "Squire Petrick's Lady" he brilliantly reduces class consciousness to the absurd of symbolism and fantasy; this forgotten short story remains his most succinct statement on the problem. The commoner wife of the story so longs to give herself to the Marquis of Christminster that she finally convinces herself she has done so. The commoner husband, hearing her vague deathbed confession that the boy Rupert is not his own son, has the interloper disinherited. But in time he develops real affection for the neglected child and even comes to feel—he who had once been wholly indifferent to aristocratic pretensions—that his wife had shown great foresight in providing the boy with such noble ancestry. The final irony occurs when he discovers from his wife's doctor that she was subject to delusions and realizes with disgust that the boy is not the Marquis of Christminster's son but his own. He bitterly observes the gradual appearance on the child's face of his own family's features rather than "the elegant knife-edged nose" of the more aristocratic line. He calls his son an impostor. All this is told in thirteen pages; the economy is that of fantasy and fable. It is irrelevant to ask whether Hardy realized how far ahead of its time this symbolic use of absurdity was. We must remember that Hardy was often most successful where least deliberate. He was capable of turning tragedy into melodrama unknowingly. He was sometimes capable, as here, of turning melodrama into symbolic tragedy.

A Group of Noble Dames, in which this story appears, is a sombre census of foolish and unhappy marriages. Only the most literal reader would suppose *Jude the Obscure,* with its attack on "indissoluble marriage" and its frank recognition of sexual incompatibility, to represent a radically new direction in thought and attitude. We know that Hardy was interested in the psychology of the epicene woman long before he created Sue Bridehead.[52] The fact is rather that various forces in the 1890's encouraged a forthright study of these problems, especially the Parnell controversy[53] and the controversy over Ibsen's plays. These were the years when one female novelist (Mrs. Golding Bright in *Virgin Soil)* could describe marriage as legalized prostitution, while another (Mrs. Oliphant) could detect the sinister machinations of an Anti-Marriage League. It is difficult to estimate what place Hardy's own marital difficulties had in the shaping of *Jude* and earlier novels, but we are forced to recognize that Hardy's "Em" and the "Em" of André Gide were frequently exasperating in the same ways: unshakably religious and conservative women who could look on their husbands' searchings for truth only with disgust and who were themselves, one gathers, of singular reticence. For whatever reasons, Hardy conceived of marriage as a dramatic illustration of the human impulse to work at cross-purposes long before he wrote *Jude the Obscure.* Far more often than not it exemplified the "circumstantial will against enjoyment" which ever frustrates the "inherent will to enjoy."[54] Few later novelists have faced this fact more honestly than Hardy did in *Jude.*

He wanted to face it honestly in earlier novels; he wanted, for instance, to suggest much more strongly that Grace Melbury had condemned herself to an unhappy marriage. But in 1886 and 1887 the censorship of "Circulating Morals" was still much too strong.[55] As early as *Desperate Remedies,* however, he had shown men and women willing to sacrifice their happiness for the sake of social position or for the sake of decent appearance. In 1882 Hardy heard the story of a woman who would not marry her seducer; he applauded her courage in refusing to become his victim a second time.[56] He dramatized this attitude—such a perverse one according to Victorian lights—several times, most notably in *The Mayor of Casterbridge* and in "For Conscience' Sake." How many of his heroines are condemned to unhappy lives for a lack of courage in the last days and hours before marriage! Fickleness, betrayal, and concealment spin nearly all of Hardy's plots—concealment of inferior social position, former lovers, illegitimate children, still-living husbands and wives. If fidelity is the most precious and elusive of the Wessex virtues, fidelity for the sake of conventional appearance and fidelity to an unworthy partner are condemned as absolutely wrong.[57] Neither the sexual act nor even the imminence of a child is in itself sufficient grounds for marriage. Charles Raye in "On the Western Circuit" duly marries the servant girl he has seduced and thereby condemns himself and her to unhappiness. The last page of this story might be the first page of a novel by Gissing.

As a writer at least, Hardy believed as strongly as did George Eliot that our every act is immortal and will eventually find us out. But he also insisted that no mechanical act of reparation can atone for or bribe the past. Marriages are not only wrecked by social ambition, prudish convention, and fickleness, but also by the dangerous assumption that a second mistake rectifies a first one. They are wrecked even more often by sheer human perversity, stubborn and incalculable—by woman's failure to persist in any course she has chosen and by her systematic preference of the most unworthy candidate, by man's obstinate allegiance to his dream of feminine perfection. Man projects his ego into space, that is, into timeless ideal illusion; woman maintains her ego in society and time. Each alike refuses to acknowledge that love has a sexual origin. "You are just like all women," Clym told Eustacia. "They are ever content to build their lives on any incidental position that offers itself; whilst men would fain make a globe to suit them." Is this the final incompatibility? In any event Hardy's true lovers find each other, like those of Dickens and Thackeray, only after they have been exhausted by life. In "The Waiting Supper" the lovers linger for seventeen years within a few hundred yards of the skeleton of the unfaithful husband who stands between them and who they daily fear will return. In our blind pursuit of happiness we blindly refuse to live.

Shall we say, then, that Hardy rigorously opposed convention and tradition—those bonds which for Conrad save the unregenerate natural man? We reach here Hardy's central area of hesitation and ambivalence, his area of conflicting sympathies.[58] Hardy frequently begins by treating his fickle Elfride Swancourts very harshly, but he ends by falling in love with them. And so too his sympathies grow for his dubious and rebellious figures—Eustacia Vye, Lucetta Le Sueur, Felice Charmond—as soon as he comes to know their suffering intimately. Is not Eustacia as justified in her longing to escape the heath as Clym in his longing to return to it? "Oh, if I had my wish," Lucetta cries, "I'd let people live and love at their pleasure." And even Felice, however badly she corrupts the Hintocks and however cosmopolitan her manners, achieves the eloquence of her creator's sympathy: "The terrible insistencies of society—how severe they are, and cold and inexorable—ghastly towards those who are made of wax and not of stone. Oh, I am afraid of them; a stab for this error, and a stab for that—correctives and regulations framed that society may tend to perfection—an end which I don't care for in the least. Yet for this, all I do care for has to be stunted and starved."[59]

The unaggressiveness of the Gabriel Oaks and the Winterbornes (and the sad end to which Jude comes) has led some critics to suppose that Hardy always disapproved the rebellious calls of instinct and divergence. Mr. Chew, for instance, makes him out to be a good Victorian humanist.[60] But no solution to the social problem was less Victorian than the one Hardy offered in 1893 to the editors of *L'Ermitage:* "I consider a social system based on individual spontaneity to promise better for happiness than a curbed and uniform one under which all temperaments are bound to shape themselves to a single pattern of living. To this end I would have society divided into *groups of tempera-*

ments, with a different code of observances for each group."[61] We may recall in this connection the wrath that falls on Angel Clare's addiction to general principles and on his inhuman power of self-mastery and the wrath that falls on even such an early prude as the highly rational Henry Knight. We do not have to wait for *Jude the Obscure* to discover Hardy's disgust with the Victorian compromise or his sympathy with those who long to escape a restricted village life. He much preferred the "passionate lover of the old-fashioned sort" to the fastidious and upright Victorian gentleman.[62]

Yet all this is in marked contradiction with much that Hardy said elsewhere. No Victorian novelist hounded his sinners and rebels to their just graves more ruthlessly. And if society should be divided into groups of temperaments, what must we say of Wessex's stabilizing virtues: its immemorial customs and taboos, its saving grace of kinship with a still-living past, its imposed conformity so absolute that the mere reading of books or the wearing of an unusual costume may cause one to be suspected of witchcraft? No doubt the stupidity of Hardy's critics led him to take more radical positions than he had ever intended; he was driven leftward in anger. But the contradiction is perhaps insoluble, as it is in many men. Hardy's distaste for the dissoluteness of London and Paris was very marked; so marked that we may almost suspect him of maintaining a double standard of morality—one code for Wessex and one for the rest of the world. In Wessex seduction and infidelity are "natural"; as natural, once again, as the seasons. But in the corrupt outside world, or when perpetrated by outsiders and aristocrats, these activities become reflective and therefore coarse and nasty. We are finally driven upon the fact, however much we resist it, that Hardy's attitude toward rural society was, like that of Wordsworth, very largely aesthetic. He could not, of course, pretend that such a narrow and secluded society encouraged spontaneity and moral independence, much as he valued these. But it did at least encourage the eccentricity which an artist could "use":

The change at the root of this has been the recent supplanting of the class of stationary cottagers, who carried on the local traditions and humours, by a population of more or less migratory labourers, which has led to a break of continuity in local history, *more fatal than any other thing to the preservation of legend, folk-lore, close inter-social relations, and eccentric individualities.* For these the indispensable conditions of existence are attachment to the soil of one particular spot by generation after generation.[63]

As the country lad who went to London to become a famous novelist, Hardy both longed for freedom and feared it. And like many of our midwestern novelists he was both attracted and repelled by the stabilities of his native region. In the end attraction proved stronger, as it so often does with literary exiles. Hardy's ideal society would be accessible to new ideas and would permit freedom to live and love, but it would simultaneously resist the passing of old customs and memories. This is a large demand and a hard bargain to drive. Hardy drove the best bargain he could with Dorset by reshaping it to his vision of Wessex.

With *Tess of the D'Urbervilles* and especially *Jude the Obscure,* Hardy left his idealized Wessex for the harsh realities and moral confusion of the modern world. Curiously enough, Hardy began and ended his career as a novelist with what were frankly problem novels. We can only surmise the exact contents of *The Poor Man and the Lady,* By the Poor Man, and it is hard to believe with Mr. Weber that the masterful and highly stylized first eight chapters of *Under The Greenwood Tree* and the spare but clumsy *Indiscretion in the Life of an Heiress* were transferred from the same now lost manuscript.[64] But we do know that this first novel included a sweeping satire of London society, the kept mistress of an architect, and even a hero who takes up radical politics! Was it any wonder that the alarmed George Meredith advised the youthful reformer to read and emulate Wilkie Collins? There is a curious link between *The Poor Man and The Lady* of 1868 and *Jude the Obscure* of 1894; in both novels a young man tells his own life story in public. (In 1865 Hardy had heard John Stuart Mill address an uncomprehending crowd in the open air.) Discouraged by this first false start, Hardy wrote in succession a superior mystery novel, a superior "rural painting of the Dutch School," and a superior romance of Lyonesse. Eventually he became, as he cynically described his ambition, "a good hand at a serial."[65] *The Hand of Ethelberta* was his closest approach before *Jude* to a sweeping satire and modern problem novel. May we surmise that he continually repressed, over twenty-five years, his impulse to add up the score of evil? If so, he more than revenged himself with *Jude the Obscure.*

Jude is an impressive tragedy, in spite of its multiplicity of separate and detachable problems. It invites enumeration of these problems—which means, of course, that they have not been absorbed by the central tragedy:

1. The socio-economic problems of educational opportunity for the poor and of class deracination.

2. The social problems of marriage, divorce, and repressive moral censorship by public opinion.

3. The psychological problems of Jude's sexuality and his urge to self-destruction, and of Sue's epicene temperament and her moral masochism.

4. The religious problem of church reforms.

5. The ethical problems of naturalistic morality and of moral sanction independent of dogma.

6. The bio-philosophical problems of inherited family characteristics and of the new will-not-to-live.

7. The spiritual problems of modern unrest, modern introspectiveness, and modern melancholy and spiritual isolation.

Some of these problems had been broached in earlier

novels, but Hardy was taking up others for the first time. And he had never before attempted to give an over-all picture of his age. At most he had looked on these things as isolated and unrelated phenomena—as unrelated as Alec D'Urberville's sexually motivated religious conversion and the economic plight of the Durbeyfields. Nor had he previously treated any of the ethical problems with depth and persistence. Tess, for instance, cuts the tightest knot of Victorian speculation with a few glib words: "She tried to argue and tell him that he had mixed in his dull brain two distinct things, theology and morals, which in the primitive days of mankind had been quite distinct, and had nothing in common but long association." Phillotson must go through a more difficult hour of ratiocination than this before he can decide to act on an instinct of kindness and "let principles take care of themselves."

Jude the Obscure remains, then, the extreme point at which we must take Hardy's measure as a "thinker." And it becomes quite clear that we must base his importance as a novelist on entirely different grounds. Hardy was nowhere wrong, as I see it, unless in his bio-philosophical determinism, but he thought neither subtly nor originally on any of these problems. Just as the Wessex novels leave an idealized impression of an ancient and stable world rather than an accurate almanac of Dorset, so *Jude the Obscure* leaves a dominant and in a sense truthful impression of the world in which we live. This impression of unrest and isolation and collapse, rather than the diverse problems discussed, makes the book still seem true. Like all self-conscious spiritual history, *Jude* has many pages which date it: Sue's discussion, for instance, of the chapter headings to the Song of Solomon. It is even conceivable that the picture of our world as rudderless and lost will some day date. But the novel will survive even this doubtful eventuality, I suspect, thanks to the rectilinear starkness and truth of Jude's personal history; the history is the truer, even, for its omission of Jude's rare happy hours.

For there will always be men willing to whisper with him: "Let the day perish wherein I was born, and the night in which it was said, There is a man child conceived."

We may pass over casually the relationship of the young Hardy to the English novel of the 1860's and 1870's. The manifest prejudices of the novel-reading public, as well as the cautionary admonitions of editors, seem to have affected Hardy far more than did contemporary fiction itself, of which he read very little. Hardy's alleged triviality of surface—his use of Gothic melodrama and coincidence—has been blamed on Ainsworth, on the popular sensation novelists who flourished after 1840, and on that very superior writer, Wilkie Collins. George Meredith has been repeatedly blamed for corrupting the young realist by sending him to Collins' books. But this does not appear to have been such bad advice to a young writer whose first novel was so autobiographical and so angry; he could have done Hardy a disservice by sending him to George Eliot or Trollope, however richer their works may be than Collins'. For Collins had exhibited a decade earlier the formula of fiction to which Hardy's talent naturally responded: the conjunction of plausible human beings and exciting, implausible, or at least uncommon circumstance. It was also the formula of fiction of George Crabbe and of the Greek dramatists.* It helped Hardy to avoid the much graver trivialities of complacent social satire and decorative higher seriousness. More reading in George Eliot and in the lesser females of the period would have encouraged Hardy's greatest weakness, his tendency to take a dogged, abstract, theoretical view of human character and situation and to diagram his chapters accordingly.

George Eliot, Meredith, Trollope, Disraeli, Collins, and

* The conjunction of "rural realism" and tragic or ironic mischance occurs in the verse tales of George Crabbe, who may be as important as Jane Austen in the development of nineteenth century realism.

Reade were towering figures when Hardy began to write; Dickens died in 1870. There were also Mrs. Oliphant, Mrs. Lynn Linton, Anne Manning, Rhoda Broughton, Charlotte Yonge, Jean Ingelow, Jessie Fothergill, Ouida, and Mary Elizabeth Braddon, who alone published sixteen novels in the seventies.[66] These are merely the names that survive (but only as names) of a most voluminous bluestocking company. Some of the titles—*Ought We to Visit Her?*, *Seducers in Ecuador*, and *The Maternity of Harriett Wicken* as against *Middlemarch* and *Daniel Deronda*—suggest an even more radical division of the reading public than exists today, and an even sharper distinction between the artist and the dispenser of sentiment. The fact is rather that even the most serious novelist then hoped for a very large public. The difference between Pearl Buck and Kathleen Norris is a difference in both talent and intention, but the difference between George Eliot and Mrs. Lynn Linton was largely a difference in talent. And there was no Victorian predecessor of Elizabeth Bowen or Katherine Anne Porter. The conception of the novelist as a complex and difficult artist writing deliberately for a trained public of ten or fifteen thousand readers simply did not exist; it scarcely existed when Conrad began writing a quarter of a century later. Charles Reade brought back from France the scissors and paste of the naturalists and even some of their frankness; but it required George Moore to bring back their intense pride in the novel as an art. In 1886 George Gissing called on Hardy for instruction in the art of fiction; Hardy was appalled, I suspect, by Gissing's willingness to immolate himself for something so dubious as the novel.[67] *New Grub Street,* with its picture of uncompromising and starving novelists, was perhaps autobiography rather than history. There were uncompromising artists among the Victorians, but they were not as a rule novelists. Hardy resolved to give up "the supply of family fiction to magazines"[68] only after he had written and mutilated *Tess*. A writer either achieved commercial success or was, as a novelist, a failure.

The effect of two- and three-volume publication (the obligation to go on at predetermined and harrowing length) is evident in Hardy's novels as in those of most of his contemporaries; it is now more glaringly evident than the supplementary effect of serial publication with its demand for periodic crises in plot. (The fact that crises recur periodically in *The Mayor of Casterbridge* is certainly less disturbing than the fact that the book is nearly a hundred pages too long.) The further obligation to write for a single incontaminate public exerted itself through the circulating libraries, but even more through the semipopular magazines. There were few magazines edited only for adults; the courageous *Fortnightly* alone was unfit for a parson's daughter's eyes. Most obviously this single genteel public could not permit the acknowledgment of sexual realities, lest youthful passions be inflamed. The Angel Clare of the serial version of *Tess* had to push the dairymaids through the puddle in a wheelbarrow instead of carrying them in his arms. Charles Reade began the fight for liberty with "The Prurient Prude," or perhaps even earlier with *Griffith Gaunt* in 1866. Twenty years later Tennyson spoke against the troughs of Zolaism in "Locksley Hall Sixty Years After," on behalf of the threatened British family. When Walter Besant said that no English woman above a certain level ever commits an indiscretion, he was guilty of determined cheerfulness, if not of willful falsehood. But the British public of 1871 actually was innocent to a rather astonishing degree. In *Desperate Remedies* there is a scene of Lesbian attachment which even today seems appalling. So inconceivable was the appearance of such a phenomenon in English life or fiction that no reader recognized it as such. Neither, very possibly, did Hardy himself.[69]

The public refusal to read about one important aspect of life may have discouraged the writing of one or two masterpieces and caused the mutilation of a few others. The hostility to pessimism was much more sinister than prudery, however, in its effect on ethics and art, as it is in any age. A multitude of sins could be forgiven the novelist who finally acknowledged that society was *fundamentally* stable and beneficent and human nature saved rather than damned. The fury aroused by *Jude the Obscure* was the fury of outraged optimism, not of outraged prudery; the book suggested that life was an unpleasant experience for all but a privileged or insensitive few and an incoherent experience for all. Popular optimism worked out a peculiar and characteristic compromise: it permitted Dickens, Reade, and others to dwell on remediable social abuses so long as they did not question the integrity of God in his Heaven and of human nature in its earthly prison, or of society as a noble experiment. This popular optimism—sentimental, as moral optimism always is—even permitted the dramatization of a great deal of suffering. For suffering aroused pity, which was tantamount to virtue. But more often this optimism assumed that the consoling view of things was the edifying one, and that the spectacle of goodness and kindness was more educative than the spectacle of evil and cruelty. In *Far from the Madding Crowd* the dog who helped the dying Fanny Robin crawl to the workhouse is driven away by stones; Hardy never wrote a more eloquent appeal for kindness to animals. A deputation of six "humanitarians" called on Hardy, however, not to thank him but to protest his cruel treatment of the dog.[70] Even *The Athenaeum* preferred *The Trumpet-Major* to *The Mayor of Casterbridge* because it recounted the tragedy of an "unselfish" rather than a "self-willed" hero.[71] Many Victorians would have preferred no tragedy at all. Charles Darwin disliked unhappy endings and wanted a law passed against them. Then as today the great enemies of art and truth were the optimists who asked to have their illusions confirmed, and the saddened who asked to be consoled for the loss of theirs.

We must take all this into account in estimating Hardy's contempt for the novel and his willingness to mutilate his books. Hardy met nearly all the great writers of his time, the Swinburnes as well as the Tennysons, but he met them generally in society. It is hard to exaggerate the triviality of the polite attitude toward literature in the 1870's and 1880's, or the triviality of the "literary life." The appalling Sir Walter Besant, and the various clubs he sponsored, suggests this triviality most strongly. One of these, the Rabelais Club, was devoted to the cause of "virility" in literature. Hardy, as the most virile writer of the time, was asked to join in 1879; Henry James was rejected as lacking in virility, though he was later invited as a guest. Such associations still exist, of course, both in England and America, but good writers do not join them. When Hardy began writing there was likewise little literary criticism which could suggest a more serious view of fiction as an art; the *Partial Portraits* of Henry James had not yet been published. Although Victorian thinkers were by no means trivial when they devoted themselves to the problems of society, economics, religion, philosophy, and science, they were nearly always trivially polite and general in their literary studies. Where was any criticism published comparable in intensity and seriousness to the Bridges-Hopkins correspondence of the period? Even the best of the literary critics in the 1860's and 1870's—Leslie Stephen, Walter Bagehot, Richard Holt Hutton, perhaps Arnold—were more interesting as critics of life than as critics of literature. When the shrewd and subtle Hutton came upon a novel that interested him (Adams' *Democracy,* for instance), he found himself without a critical vocabulary with which to describe it. Criticism was rich in grand general statements about the relationships of literature and life, form and content, etc., but it rarely got down to particulars. Arnold's only procedure for getting down to particulars was to list individual passages which moved him; even he seldom discussed the structure of feeling in an entire poem. And so critics might intuitively recognize *Under the Greenwood Tree* to be a fine novel, yet have no way of knowing why it was so. More often they preferred the worst books, *The Trumpet-Major* in particular. They were almost unanimous in their dislike of *The Return of the Native.*

Thus Hardy could learn little of value from the criticism of the day, and it is perhaps as well that he read so little contemporary fiction. Shakespeare, Sophocles, and even George Crabbe were more to his purpose than Meredith, Trollope, and George Eliot, each of whom might have imposed an alien formula. We may also be thankful that Meredith sent Hardy back to Wilkie Collins rather than to Dickens. For Dickens, certainly the greatest creative talent of the century in England, was a most difficult influence to digest;* it was better for Hardy to work toward the grotesque, macabre, and symbolic independently. On the other hand, Hardy was rather too receptive to personal advice. He blundered into fiction because he could not get his poems published, and he looked to publishers' readers and editors for instruction. Meredith's suggestion led to the melodrama of *Desperate Remedies,* Morley's praise of a country scene led to the ruralism of *Under the Greenwood Tree,* Stephen's demand for more action led to the complex plotting of *Far from the Madding Crowd,* the critical insistence on his pastoral qualities drove him by reaction to *The Hand of Ethelberta.* "Thus," as Granville Hicks remarks, "Hardy was nearly forty years old and the author of five novels before he ceased trying to shape his work according to somebody else's interpretation of what the public wanted."[72] And in the years that followed he was quite willing to suppress what, according to editors, the public did not want. Similarly he took Miss Thacke-

*Undigested Dickens is to be found in English and American fiction through the second half of the century; it overlies and sometimes almost suppresses native talent. Consider, for instance, its anomalous appearance in Melville's *Bartleby the Scrivener.* It appears notably in the coyness of the rustics in *Under the Greenwood Tree* and *Far from the Madding Crowd.*

ray's word that a novelist must move in society, and duly took notes on his dismal findings there.

Hardy resolved to give up writing fiction when *Under the Greenwood Tree* was rejected, and again after the rejection of *Tess*. How can we reconcile the greatness of Hardy's talent with his apparent indifference to fiction as an art, with his bowdlerizations, with his "wish merely to be considered a good hand at a serial" even after *Far from the Madding Crowd?*[73] We must accept literally, I think, his reiterated preference for his poetry, and in some respects this preference was justified. On the other hand there is scarcely a novel which does not unmistakably reveal creative energy and creative delight: a naïve and primitive concern with the fate of his characters, a joy in imagined and grotesque circumstance, a pleasure in phrasing and shaping, a radical submergence of self in the thing being made. The delight which he took was the delight of the child in his mother's stories—those popular stories which were, perhaps, the first "source" of his work. But to the poet and scientist in sound who worked out skeleton verse patterns for poems without words, this delight may have seemed primitive and unworthy. There is also the fact that his novels, though colored by temperament as markedly as the poems, are much less autobiographical and subjective than they.

Thus the facts of Hardy's life are very nearly as irrelevant to an understanding of his novels as the literary tendencies of the age; we look largely in vain for a figure in the carpet of fact. At the age of fifty Hardy went to the Moulin Rouge to see women dance the cancan, but he saw instead the Montmartre cemetery "through some back windows over their heads."[74] How shall we say how much the macabre imagination of the novelist owed to the child of Bockhampton who saw a woman hung for murder? Hardy did not dramatize and study his actual life with the microscopic anxiety of Gide, nor did he identify himself with any character in the way that Conrad identified himself with Marlow, Heyst, and Decoud. He was not by nature a directly subjective novelist, as the opening chapters of *A Pair of Blue Eyes* show. For these chapters—which reproduce in some detail his great Cornish romance, the journey into Lyonesse of such intensely personal poems—are among the coldest and least energized in the book. Thereafter Hardy seldom used his personal experience so directly. Nor did he, so far as we can discern with any certainty, use his novels to liquidate personal anxieties: fear, remorse, or guilt. We can, for instance, attach no single page in his writing to the highly interesting fact that all his life he disliked being touched.[75] Vacant places remain even in the formal biography of this outwardly simple and prosaic man. His years in London between 1862 and 1867, when he seems to have lost his remaining faith, were perhaps as important as the London years of the young Wordsworth, but for essentials they remain nearly as obscure. They were enjoyable years, the second Mrs. Hardy tells us, but they were no doubt more than that. She also tells us that Hardy, though sensitive to criticism, was not given to introspection; was, in fact, very little interested in himself.[76] He seems to have had that capacity for depersonalized sympathy to which Gide laid claim but as a novelist rather conspicuously lacked. This depersonalization may explain in part the singular woodenness of Hardy's men, with the exception of Henchard, Jude, and perhaps a very few others.

A strong undercurrent of melancholy and nostalgia runs through all the novels; there is, at another extreme, the unrelaxed consciousness and resentment of class feeling. But behind these most general and familiar leanings we find very few signs of particular eccentricity, very few highly individual obsessions. The most interesting of these seem to be a fascinated attitude toward women regarded as *objects* (that is, in terms of personality), an unusually marked consciousness of sexual infidelity and betrayal, and above all a preoccupation with men who exhibit a curious unaggressiveness of character. The fascination of women as God's most perverse and delightful mysteries reminds one of Richardson. Like Richardson, Hardy as a youth wrote love letters for the illiterate, and like Richardson he was always comfortably surrounded by women.[77] His diary is full of jottings on the personalities of the women he met—and on the intellectual convictions of the men. At fifty he retained his youthful delight in circuses, dancing, and music, and took an incorrigible pleasure in going to music halls and in visiting girls' schools. Should we go back to the child of eleven who fiddled at country dances sometimes through the whole night, watching the Anna Barretts and the Esther Olivers whirl mysteriously by, and who was hopelessly in love with the *grande dame* of the parish? Even as an old man he recalled the names of the "bevy now underground," young women about twenty when he was a child.[78]

It would be dangerous to put much personal emphasis on Hardy's concern with sexual betrayal, infidelity, and concealment. For these, at the origin of much tragedy anywhere, glare more distinctly in small and isolated communities and are likely to furnish the greatest part of any rural drama. They are also inevitably the stock in trade of a novelist who depends heavily on plot. May they not also signify, for the novelist concerned with larger human meanings, the very first human fact—that we all have something to conceal? Even when we have made these reservations, however, Hardy's census of betrayal remains exceptionally full and detailed. There is little to be learned from an enumeration of true lovers thrown over or of illegitimate children and hasty marriages concealed. The most interesting clue (if it is a clue) lies in the shifting role of the woman from that of the fickle betrayer to that of the simple-hearted betrayed, from Fancy Day and Elfride Swancourt to Marty South and Tess. Even Elfride finally wins her creator's sympathy, but we have to wait for *Two on a Tower* to find an unequivocal heroine more sinned against than sinning. The balance first begins to tip in *Far from the Madding Crowd,* where Bathsheba changes from the vain and fickle punisher of Gabriel Oak to the frank and resourceful manager of the farm, betrayed by Sergeant Troy. In Thomasin Yeobright we have the first of several innocent victims whose only flaw is a lack of judgment. But who could be expected to love Diggory Venn, who so obstinately refuses to live; whose function is to watch others live and very occasionally to "meddle"?

Hardy's immaturity, according to the second Mrs. Hardy, "was greater than is common for his years, and it may be mentioned here that a clue to much of his character and action throughout his life is afforded by his lateness of development in virility, while mentally precocious."[79] Does this explain Jude's similarly late development? Is it above all a clue to the singular unaggressiveness of Gabriel Oak, John Loveday, Giles Winterborne, and so many others; even of Diggory Venn, who is no less significant here because he was intended to be a symbolic and mysterious outsider? The amount of shy onlooking in Hardy—of peeping and overhearing, of willing renunciation, of symbolic satisfaction gained through arranging the fortunes of others and through watching others live—is wholly out of proportion with its classical usefulness as a device of plot. The characteristic Hardy hero treads a path near the loved one's house, hoping to catch a glimpse of her, or he stares through lighted windows or fondles old letters. If Boldwood is the only passive observer to become markedly neurotic, many of the others cherish their suffering. And nearly all of them, from Stephen Smith and Henry Knight to Angel Clare, cause suffering through their passiveness. We shall have to return to these characters; we shall have to distinguish between the unambitious farmers, the overreflective intellectuals and prudes, the stoics, and the demonic unsexed spectators of tragedy. Hardy himself was exceptionally unambitious,[80] and he undoubtedly admired the unselfishness of Winterborne and Oak. His attitude toward other forms of passiveness—toward sexual passiveness in particular—is ambiguous where it is not frankly critical. At least once he denounced the reticent and self-controlled Victorian lover directly, as a sad diminution from the "passionate lover of the old-fashioned sort." Havelock Ellis was disturbed by these "pale and featureless" men. When he observed that men of the Wilhelm Meister and Daniel Deronda class were his favorite heroes, Hardy replied, "I think you are only saying in another way that these men are the modern man—the type to which the great mass of educated modern men are assimilating more or less."[81] Mr. Chew finds grounds in these unaggressive men for "the optimism of Thomas Hardy."[82] It would be more accurate to consider them direct expressions of the temperamental pessimism, of the total vision of loneliness and of man's perverse refusal to live. The Devil, who appeared to Gide in his classic guise of the *raisonneur,* may also appear as the spectator, the voyeur, who participates not in life. But we cannot be sure that Hardy saw this to be so.

The personal portrait which Mrs. Hardy left us is that of a kindly, fun-loving, and extraordinarily simple man, who lacked even the energizing forces of Wordsworth's introspectiveness and vanity. But kindly, fun-loving, and simple men do not write great novels and poems, however traditional in content; something is plainly lacking to the portrait. What this is a definitive biography will have to infer, I suspect, from the novels and poems themselves, remembering always that the simplest personalities may be the most difficult to explain. Hardy himself, who once said he would give ten years of his life to see a real ghost, left at least two important clues to his personality and art. Very possibly he had the great gift of being able to stand simultaneously inside and outside everyday life. The first passage dates from 1915, the second from 1887:

Half my time—particularly when writing verse—I "believe" (in the modern sense of the word) not only in the things

Bergson believes in, but in spectres, mysterious voices, intuitions, omens, dreams, haunted places, etc., etc. But I do not believe in them in the old sense of the word any more for that.

I was thinking a night or two ago that people are somnambulists—that the material is not the real—only the visible, the real being invisible optically. That is because we are in a somnambulistic hallucination that we think the real to be what we see as real.[83]

CONFLICTING IMPULSES

THE CRITIC OFTEN GOES TO THE BIOGrapher for clues to the work of art when it would be more logical for the biographer to go to the work of art and to the critic for clues to the living man. Not the most intimate biographical record, for instance, could tell us as much about Dostoevsky as his novels tell us. Analytic biography and the analysis of literary form must depend alike and at last on the creative impulses actually exhibited and the pattern which has been made of these impulses. What prompted and impelled the novelist must finally be discovered by a reading of his books.

Some novelists may be impelled only by a need to understand their own experience. Their books represent a facing down of the menace of life; or, if you like, an uninterrupted race against madness, degradation, and suicide. Others may be obsessed more particularly—with the ubiquity of suffering, with the invasion of mind by natural animal process, or with the corruptness of politicians—and their sole creative impulse (whether they know it or not) is to see and make us see these things. But normally the novelist is driven by various and even contradictory impulses; then the problem of form becomes far more difficult, both for him and for the critic. A Thomas Wolfe, for instance, may be all but overpowered by the violence of the contradictions, while a Conrad manages to exploit that violence and reduce it to some semblance of order. Conrad was a teller of tales, but also a realist who wanted to record a passing way of life, a psychologist curious as to motives and the reality lurking behind appearance, and a technician experimenting with forms. He was also impelled by a demonic urge to express his nihilism and by a moralist's urge to define, intellectually, the dread consequences of that nihilism. Yet he managed to make of these singularly divergent impulses—some of them conscious, some not—a fairly coherent body of work. He contrived to express a final vision of things; he managed to forge a style.

Hardy's impulses as a novelist, beyond the very noticeable one of wanting to make a living, were even more numerous and divergent than Conrad's, and they did not always work together in harmony. Hardy was primarily a teller of tales, longing both to create life rather than merely record it and to hold the reader enthralled. He was also to some degree a psychologist, though impelled less by curiosity than sympathy. He was certainly at times a realist in the several senses of the word. He wanted to describe ordinary human beings; he wanted to speculate on their dilemmas rationally and even schematically; and he wanted to record his pious memory of the material universe, of *things* touched and tasted and seen. As an artist, he wanted to construct shapely forms which had their own intrinsic beauty. Occasionally he felt the impulse to comedy (in all its detached coldness) as well as the impulse to farce, but he was more often impelled to see tragedy and record it—the irony of misplaced longing, of energy misdirected, of consciousness overpowered. Finally, he wanted to be more than a realist. He wanted to escape the banality of exact observation and to express his particular awareness of the grotesque, the occult, and the strange. He was determined to see a ghost.

These various impulses were sacrificed to each other inevitably and often. "Inevitably," because Hardy did not care in the way that Flaubert or James or Gide cared, and sometimes took paths of least resistance. Thus one impulse often surrendered to a fresher one and, instead of exacting a compromise, simply disappeared. A desire to throw over reality a light that never was might give way abruptly to the poet-scientist's desire to record exactly the structure and texture of a flower. Here at least one form of intense pressure was substituted for another without noticeable relaxation of style. But frequently Hardy abandoned a perilous and thus highly energizing impulse (the impulse to cool comedy, for instance) in favor of what was for him the fatally relaxing impulse to theorize, classify, and schematize. When this occurred, his style—that sure index to literary character—became woolly and diffuse. Hardy's formal weakness derived from his apparent inability to control the comings and goings of these divergent impulses and from his unwillingness to cultivate and sustain the harsher ones. He submitted to first one then another, and the spirit blew where it listed. Hence the radical unevenness not merely of his work as a whole but of any one book. His most controlled novel, *Under the Greenwood Tree,* is the product of the two different but reconcilable impulses of the folk-historian and the psychologist of love, but an attitude of playful sympathy and the slight interlockings of plot are not enough to bind the two together. Thus even this book splits into two distinct parts. In all his other novels we may point to whole chapters where the shaping artist, instead of resisting uncomfortable pressures, submitted to them; where he sacrificed energy to repose. For an impulse to which we submit passively is nearly always uncreative.

We shall find, then, that some of Hardy's impulses as

a novelist were harmfully relaxing, whereas others provoked an energizing, animating tension and forced him to explore actively and work under hard rewarding pressure. The problem of pressure cannot be reduced, however, to the problem of surmounted difficulty, of resistance to easy inclination. Conrad recorded the lonely anguish which *Nostromo* and *Heart of Darkness* cost him; the less interesting *Rescue* merely puzzled him and so refused to advance. Similarly Gide's great *L'Immoraliste* was the product of anguished self-exploration and discovery, whereas the dull *Ecole des femmes,* which cost him more pains than any other book, proceeded from a then sterilizing impulse to analyze the social question. Some impulses are thus more valuable than others, and their value varies according to the particular novelist's temperament. When Conrad attempts some final general statement on human nature, his mind is excited to a very high energizing pressure and distinction; when Hardy so speculates, his style relaxes and he mumbles platitudes.

In a general way the distribution of energy and impulse also affects the total structure of the book. Let us say, at the risk of laboring the obvious, that there are three forces to be kept in harmony: the animating impulse or impulses, the human circumstances observed, and the number of pages in the book. In most novels the characters depart from one point of equilibrium, are affected by various adventures, and arrive at another point of equilibrium. (These may also be, of course, points of equilibrium in the novelist's conception of his characters.) Ideally the animating impulse—to unmask motives, for instance—should not exhaust itself before the plot has achieved its final equilibrium, and when this equilibrium has been achieved, the book should come to an end physically. Hardy frequently mismanages this most general kind of structure; partly, of course, because he was writing to roughly predetermined length. Some of his books refuse to get started, most notably *The Trumpet-Major;* others, like *The Woodlanders,* come to a definite conclusion and have to be awkwardly restarted. Any reader can detect these failings and the disturbing divergence of what should be parallel lines. We may take *Desperate Remedies* as a single extreme example.

In the ninety pages of the first five chapters no really animating impulse is at work, or, if there, is stifled by the beginner's very manifest difficulties; we follow the languid trials of a colorless young couple in love. The book recovers energy in the sixth chapter with the appearance of a highly abnormal woman, Miss Aldclyffe; the next few chapters are animated by Hardy's curiosity concerning her motives and those of Aeneas Manston, a Byronic if not diabolic villain. Then an entirely new impulse, that of the architect and minute observer, energizes the astonishing tenth chapter about the fire, and the motive-seeking psychologist is suppressed. In the ensuing chapters we return to the love story of Edward Springrove and Cytherea Graye, which reaches an unhappy conclusion in the middle of the thirteenth chapter. Forty additional pages, however, provide a happy resolution of their difficulties, and the book comes to a second and now full stop. But one hundred and thirty-five pages remain; these are animated by a sheer delight in ingenious detection and by a frank delight in the macabre. There is no discernible relationship between Hardy's shifting impulses as a novelist, the fortunes of the main characters, and the actual length of the book. *Desperate Remedies* remains a better novel than is commonly assumed, but it does so in spite of the fact that it is not one novel but three or four.

Several critics have dismissed the problem of Hardy's unevenness by casual references to his "evil genius" or "demon" of plot, and to his fondness for bizarre ironies; they see him as a realist corrupted by the age. There is of course some truth in this simple view of a rather complex matter. Ingenious and contrived plotting may be entirely accomplished during the outline and work-sheet stage of composition; the energy generated there may or may not carry over to the exploratory act and art of writing. The planning and execution of a complicated or melodramatic plot may enervate rather than excite; it may even take the entire place of a genuinely creative impulse, may provide a comfortable and relaxing substitute. This is certainly what occurred after the fine opening sections of *Two on a Tower* and *A Laodicean,* and what perhaps occurred in the last hundred pages of *Far from the Madding Crowd* and in five chapters of *The Mayor of Casterbridge.*[84] The crowded plotting may be a symptom of fatigue. In several other novels, however, exactly the opposite is true. In these books the impulse to fantastic or elaborate plotting is in fact an impulse to create life or express an attitude, and as such is highly energizing.

A Pair of Blue Eyes, for instance, is rescued after nearly two hundred pages of drably competent realism by the arrival of Henry Knight—to whom Elfride must perforce tell lies. Elfride almost immediately falls off the church tower and fifty pages further on Knight is suspended on the Cliff without a Name, "in the presence of a personalized loneliness." Thereafter, his energies now fully aroused, Hardy can force his characters to subserve a sustained vision of irony, of life working at cross-purposes. The initial melodrama both animated and made credible this view of life as essentially grotesque. *The Hand of Ethelberta* is almost saved after one hundred and ninety pages of lifeless satire by a radical change in Hardy's conception of the heroine, by her passage from a witty poetess to a grasping and indomitable head of a family, determined that her brood shall survive. But this interesting conception is soon submerged in further lifeless satire, and the book is finally saved—if saved at all—by a very melodramatic conclusion. Will the various rescuers rushing through a stormy night arrive in time to save Ethelberta from marriage with Mountclere? Will she, sadder and wiser, escape him on the wedding night? For the first time, and after four hundred pages, the book seems thoroughly alive.

So too *The Trumpet-Major* is lifeless until Bob Loveday and his dubious fiancée Mathilda arrive and provoke various complications in plot. For what can one do with a heroine whose only virtue is discretion? After its initial collapse, *A Laodicean* is the dreariest of Hardy's novels, but it too is redeemed at the last by the hilariously absurd plotting of the final chapters: Paula Power's pursuit across Normandy of her very retiring lover. In each of these books sheer delight in contrivance created energy, and this energy succeeded in animating till then lifeless characters. But melodrama can also serve to establish a convention of feeling and make the miraculous credible. So the very quality of its melodrama, the gratuitousness of its opening chapters, should convince us that *The Romantic Adventures of a Milkmaid* is a fairy story in which not merely anything can happen, but in which anything should. The highly implausible appearance of the Baron's sinister coach makes plausible the later appearance of a demon lover's yacht.

It is dangerous, of course, to describe dogmatically the physics of creative energy. What appears to be surrender to fatigue may actually be surrender to what the public presumably wanted in the way of a theatrical or consoling ending. We know that Hardy altered his original plan for *The Return of the Native* (which would have left Diggory Venn isolated and "mysterious") in deference to his tender-minded public; the same cynicism was responsible for the ending of *The Woodlanders* and may have been responsible for the ending of *Far from the Madding Crowd.* The conclusions of Victorian novels so often have nothing to do with the novels themselves that we must look to earlier chapters for significant instances of abandoned or perverted impulse. *A Laodicean* and *Two on a Tower* offer the clearest instances to be found in Hardy. In the case of *A Laodicean* we know at least one reason for the surrender. Shortly after beginning the serial version, Hardy suffered an internal hemorrhage and had to dictate the rest of the book from his sickbed through five painful months. Our knowledge of this circumstance makes the example more rather than less interesting. It permits us to define what constituted for Hardy the easy ways out; what kinds of impulse he abandoned or cultivated when subjected to severe personal stress. An exceedingly difficult detached manner is abandoned for an easier but still energizing impulse to suggest preternatural intervention, but this in turn is abandoned for the even more relaxing medium of the drably realistic travelogue.

The first book of *A Laodicean* is a study of Jamesian nuances, told in the manner of Edith Wharton; it would be hard to overestimate the pains this manner must have cost. George Somerset, a young architect and the most convincing of Hardy's intellectuals, stumbles upon the interesting ambiguity of Paula Power, a railroad magnate's very modern daughter who owns the castle of the declined De Stancys and who has a Laodicean tenderness for both the new and the old. She wants to manufacture pottery and industrialize the community and she delights in her personal telegraph machine, but also she longs to be an ancient and conservative De Stancy. It is Somerset's bored exploring curiosity and the fascination of ambiguity which prompt him to fall in love; his love in turn threatens to corrupt his architectural principles. Hero and heroine approach each other through evasiveness; their allegiance to illusion is brilliantly and economically defined at the garden party where they are separated from the dancing guests by a sudden and gauzy rain:

> . . . the rain streaming down between their eyes and the lighted interior of the marquee like a tissue of glass threads, the brilliant forms of the dancers passing and repassing behind the watery screen, as if they were people in an enchanted submarine palace.[85]

So separated from reality (which to them seems illusion),

the practical Paula can almost admit to Somerset that she loves him.

Thus are established, through one hundred and forty pages, the materials for a minute psychological comedy of temperamental differences. But the difficulties facing the lovers were as nothing compared to those which faced the novelist, who would have had to explore each subtle change in detail while sustaining an unaccustomed point of view (*i.e.,* attitude). He therefore abandoned the social ambiguities of Paula for the preternatural ambiguities of William Dare. The impulse to suggest that this prodigious youth was in fact a supernatural being, a "Mephistophelian visitant," was an energizing though here somewhat frivolous one; it gave some strength to the short second book.[86] For to show the Devil circulating incognito among plausible moderns was, as Gide later discovered in the *Faux-monnayeurs,* no easy task. The task proved in fact so difficult that Hardy abandoned it after forty pages and revealed Dare to be nothing more unnatural than Captain De Stancy's natural son. At this point, with the second of its animating impulses abandoned, the book collapses completely. The symptom of collapse is, as nearly always with Hardy, woolly abstract summarizing,[87] and in addition the appearance of a grotesquely theoretical psychology. Captain De Stancy, remorseful because he had abandoned Dare's mother, had become a monster of self-discipline. But a drink and the sight of Paula in her pink flannel gymnasium suit awaken the old Adam at once. Confronted by such an implausible human being, the interesting Paula becomes a model of Victorian prudence; thus can one poor character corrupt another. Even the impulse of a highly abstract curiosity concerning motives is now abandoned, and Paula and De Stancy depart on what is surely the dullest European journey in all fiction. There are few clearer instances than this one of a novelist abandoning in succession all the interesting—and difficult—possibilities of his subject. Two hundred and fifty drab pages precede the return of genuine comedy in Paula's absurd pursuit of Somerest through the cathedral towns and beach resorts of Normandy.

Two on a Tower displays a lapse of creative energy almost as striking, and the abandonment of a difficult but highly rewarding impulse. The first hundred pages offer, surprisingly, a cool high comedy in the French manner, an amusing study of preoccupied self-delusion. Swithin St. Cleeve is a prodigious astronomer who looks on Lady Viviette Constantine as a disinterested patroness of science. She, aging and lonely, is even more deluded than he; at most she acknowledges to herself a few maternal feelings. The reader of *The Return of the Native* would hardly imagine Hardy capable of such urbane irony. The seventh chapter—in which Lady Constantine detains the young scientist by offering him an equatorial telescope for his tower and a whole pheasant for his lunch, and later by asking him astronomical questions which require lengthy answers—might well have been written by Stendhal. Lord David Cecil attributes the weakness of *Two on a Tower* to the fact that its theme, the "contrast between the stellar universe and human passion," deserved no more than a lyric.[88] But this contrast is in no important sense the theme or subject of the novel. The real subject, the conflict of mature and youthful temperament, is abandoned almost as soon as it has been masterfully established, at the moment when Lady Constantine and St. Cleeve recognize they love each other even more than the stars. Lady Constantine's first husband had long since disappeared and is presumably dead. The lovers are free to marry; the introduction to the book is complete.

These then were the materials for a comedy of manners which would require the most severely maintained control: a disparity in age and temperament which would sooner or later betray itself and a mismarriage to scandalize the neighborhood between an unclassed adolescent and the *grande dame* of the parish. The comedy would require, of course, that its victims remain side by side, as they had been on their observation tower. But the task of sustaining such a subject, and his own attitude of ironic detachment, was more than Hardy could face. He therefore introduced a complicated series of external obstacles: Lady Constantine's ambitious brother, a will which required St. Cleeve not to marry before he was twenty-five, an impetuous bishop, and the news that Lady Constantine's first husband had died later than she thought. Each of these obstacles, which determined first that St. Cleeve and Lady Constantine marry secretly and then that their marriage be no marriage, helped Hardy avoid the difficult ironic mood he had maintained so brilliantly at first; helped him evade his real subject, the temperamental clash. The final surrender to mere pathos occurs with St. Cleeve's departure for Cambridge, Massachusetts, and other distant parts days only before Lady Constantine discovers she is pregnant. Her immediate marriage with the Bishop of Melchester scandalized Hardy's early readers by its immorality and scandalizes us by its virtuous appeal to tears. Lady Constantine, who had been so engaging, becomes a sacrificed and sacrificing victim. In due time the moralizing Bishop dies; St. Cleeve returns; the now distinctly aged Lady Constantine dies on top of the tower from the shock of joy; Tabitha Lark, presumably the future Mrs. St. Cleeve, bounds youthfully across the field below. But long since, at the very moment in fact of his first evasion, Hardy's prose style had become flabby and abstract.[89] Pity, which often threatens to undermine Hardy's tragedies but rarely does so, here vitiated the most promising of his comedies. The pity was an easy and relaxing substitute for hard ironic curosity, the real animating impulse of the book.

In both *A Laodicean* and *Two on a Tower* Hardy abandoned an unfamiliar and stimulating manner at the very moment this manner became most difficult—and most likely to pay the high reward of difficulty. The price and symptom of this fatigued evasion was a sudden relaxation of style and an immediate recourse to contrivance in psychology and plot. Such evasions occur, though rarely so blatantly, in even the best of his novels. A slightly different form of evasion—the use of contrived psychology to prepare a tragic or pathetic situation—similarly betrays itself at once through abrupt changes in style; Hardy seemingly could not be dishonest with impunity. The crucial interview between Henchard and Newson in *The Mayor of Casterbridge* (Chapter 41) offers a very clear instance of this.

The four preceding chapters had accelerated Henchard's decline at a rather alarming rate, either because Hardy was getting tired or because he had exhausted his feelings about these scenes before he came to write them.[90] Within fifty pages Henchard had conquered his impulse to reveal Lucetta as the author of the love letters and had agreed to return the letters to her; he had been disgraced on the occasion of the royal visit and had had his fight with Farfrae; Jopp had read the letters and initiated the skimmington ride; Lucetta, as a result of her public disgrace, had died after an epileptic fit; and Henchard, in the loneliness of guilt, had recovered his old affection for Elizabeth-Jane. At this point of equilibrium—when conceivably Henchard could have settled down to a life of unvindictive retirement—the sailor Newson, Elizabeth-Jane's real father, returns and demands to see her. Henchard at once says she is dead; Newson immediately believes him and walks away without asking embarrassing questions.

Few readers have not deplored Newson's quite unexpected reappearance; and the reappearance is certainly managed clumsily. It can be justified symbolically, however. For it is the very convention of this tragedy that every ghost of our past life must return to confront us at last; that it is impossible to lay a ghost; that the ghost inhabits us in the form of a self-destructive urge. The furmity-woman is a real woman, but she is also an ineradicable part of Henchard's mind. The essential dishonesty or contrivance consists in the behavior of Henchard and Newson during the interview, not in the fact of Newson's reappearance. That Henchard should have lied immediately and unreflectively is at least conceivable; that Newson should have gone away without asking for some details of his daughter's life is, in view of his long-standing ambition to take care of her, wholly preposterous. I suspect that Hardy, subconsciously at least, considered both reactions improbable. In any event he felt obliged to explain these reactions in commonplace and dogged prose. Creative energy, the energy which derives from a valuable and honest impulse, is more conspicuously lacking in these pages than anywhere else in the book.[91]

I have spoken of cultivation and suppression of creative impulse, of resistance and surrender, and even of honesty and dishonesty, as though the artist were responsible at every moment for the forces which prompt him; as though he were always the initiator of impulse, as well as its beneficiary. This is of course an absurdity which the shortcuts of language compel. It would perhaps be more exact to speak of the artist as the guardian and censor of creative impulse and to say that responsibility lies in his more or less clear awareness of what he happens to be about, and in his consequent supervision of self. Conceivably a novelist could take an ironic and detached attitude toward his characters unknowingly; but it is hard to imagine him (unless neurotic or insane) remaining in ignorance indefinitely. It is certainly impossible to determine at every given point whether evasion was deliberate or not. There is good reason to believe, on the other hand, that in *A Laodicean* and *Two on a Tower* Hardy clearly foresaw the difficulty of remaining ironic and detached, and understood that there were other and easier ways out. In the final analysis, the degree of deliberateness is irrelevant.

Subconscious evasion (uneasiness or creative apathy in the face of undefined difficulties) may be as strong as conscious surrender and often even more harmful. When a novelist abandons a difficult manner he may be acting with wise foresight; or in laziness, cowardice, or ignorance.

The problem presents itself to a highly subjective novelist in a relatively simple form; his perils are enormous but comparatively few in number. Though a subjective poet, Hardy was not a subjective novelist in the sense that Conrad and André Gide were. His impulses were often rudimentary but also highly diverse; he was multiform as well as primitive. Two of these impulses, the realist and the anti-realist, offer the most extreme instance of diversity; a contrast more striking than that of the comic and tragic attitudes. On the one hand Hardy wanted to remain faithful to reason, to ordinary experience, to things. On the other hand he wanted to see and create beyond them. His determination to transcend ordinary realism is the one which must chiefly interest the modern novelist, who is similarly engaged. But we must first take into brief account the realist who appealed to an earlier generation: the architectonic craftsman who paced out the number of steps his characters took across the heath, the rationalist who coldly schematized their dilemmas, the observer who recorded their evanescent customs and their unchanging natural environment.

The realist is in one sense a rationalist, not merely because he speculates on experience but also because he seeks to impose the order of his mind on the fluid and seemingly brute disorder of that experience. He accomplishes this through literary form, which is both the medium and the end product of perception; through the very act of shaping he comes to understand what he shapes. Thomas Mann, obviously, and Marcel Proust, more indirectly, offer striking examples of rational realism: of the penetration and ordering of an immense chaos through the agency of shaping mind, of assimilating not assimilated form. Only the most unregenerate surrealist would deplore their triumphs. For the novelist's extreme alternative to this process is submergence in the shapelessness of experience not understood; even Joyce falls back on and exploits a substructure of theory and myth. It is necessary to acknowledge thus the unequivocal virtue of form in the novel even as we deplore Hardy's marked architectonic impulse. There is of course no paradox here, for though Hardy diagrammed his plots, cultivated the unities and exactitudes, and so forth, he was, as we have seen, very indifferent to the major concerns of form: timing, the control of tone and attitude, the distribution of energy and creative impulse. His very concern with the most mechanical aspects of form seems to have distracted his attention from these essentials. He even thought of form as superadded ornament, as a decorative addition to content.[92]

Hardy, who was once regarded as a slovenly, reckless, and uneducated craftsman in verse, long experimented with new metrical forms, and sometimes worked out "verse skeletons": either nonsense verses written to a predetermined formula or wordless patterns of stanza, accent, and, according to Mrs. Hardy, quantity.[93] Perhaps his object was, like that of Hopkins and Bridges, to reinvigorate or replace forms which seemed exhausted. Mrs. Hardy's spare allusions to these skeletons suggest, however, that he regarded them as so many vessels to be filled by the words of a real poem; that he did not meditate—though he now and then masterfully exemplified—the relationship of meter to perception. In this he was of course very different from Hopkins and Bridges, and it is not surprising to find that his best poems are those most traditional in form, whereas some of the most elaborately wrought meters have little relationship to the feeling of the poems. His experimentation thus recalls that of Tennyson and Swinburne, who so often looked on metrical form as a musical beauty to be added to content. So too with his speculations on the language of poetry. He was dissatisfied with Wordsworth's classification in the 1815 preface to the *Poems,* but himself produced a scheme almost as preposterous for determining the proper language to be used in "fanciful," "meditative," "sentimental," and "passionate" verse.[94] Hardy was a great poet, even a great master of form and language, but in spite of such triviality as this. His human poetic intelligence was considerable; his academic poetic intelligence was commonplace.

It is unnecessary to quarrel with the fact that Hardy pored over a road map, which he had duly marked with distances, while composing *The Return of the Native;* his imagination was sufficient to overcome this topographical pedantry and the handicap of visualization so exact. The formal commonplaceness betrays itself rather in the tendency to group characters in highly artificial counterpoint. It is no wonder that Hardy's critics have so often been tempted to chart the algebra of "concatanated affections" in *The Return of the Native, The Woodlanders,* and *The Mayor of Casterbridge;* some such charts very obviously guided Hardy's hand. *Far from the Madding Crowd* suffers more than any of the other novels from this mechanical arrangement; there are many passages like the following:

> And Troy's deformities lay deep down from a woman's vision, whilst his embellishments were upon the very surface; thus contrasting with homely Oak, whose defects were patent to the blindest, and whose virtues were as metals in a mine.[95]

The principle of counterpoint was also applied to the inner debate of each character in turn. No doubt the impulse to see things in this way, as well as the reading of eighteenth-century essayists, accounts for the annoying mannerism of style which appears through the first half of this book:

> She moved between them as a chaise between carts, was heard

after them as a romance after sermons, was felt among them like a breeze among furnaces.

Bathsheba's was an impulsive nature under a deliberative aspect. An Elizabeth in brain and a Mary Stuart in spirit, she often performed actions of the greatest temerity with a manner of extreme discretion. Many of her thoughts were perfect syllogisms; unluckily they always remained thoughts.

Bathsheba, though she had too much understanding to be entirely governed by her womanliness, had too much womanliness to use her understanding to the best advantage. . .

Bathsheba loved Troy in the way that only self-reliant women love when they abandon their self-reliance. When a strong woman recklessly throws away her strength she is worse than a weak woman who has never had any strength to throw away.[96]

Jude the Obscure was intended to be Hardy's great masterpiece of contrapuntal structure, as one of his letters tells us; he regretted that more reviewers did not discern his abstract pattern:

Of course the book is all contrasts—or was meant to be in its original conception. Alas, what a miserable accomplishment it is!—e.g. Sue and her heathen gods set against Jude's reading the Greek testament; Christminster academical, Christminster in the slums; Jude the saint, Jude the sinner; Sue the Pagan, Sue the saint; marriage, no marriage; etc. etc.[97]

The modern reader discerns these and other contrasts only too clearly, however, and marvels that the book manages to survive its almost geometrical construction; that all the characters but Little Father Time transcend the formulae so carefully laid out. For Hardy's impulse to group his plots and characters contrapuntally was also, notably, an impulse to present dilemmas didactically. He thought coldly and conceptually about his characters; the commonplaceness of his thought struggled persistently with his dramatic or poetic talent. In every novel we stumble unexpectedly upon signs of the struggle: an undigested idea, an undramatized contrast, an unconcealed and grossly abstract intention. We stumble, in brief, upon the naked presence of Hardy's original outline—which means, of course, that he has not thought hard enough.

The struggle can be discerned most easily in the poems, where the invasion of the moral by the didactic usually betrays itself at once.[98] On November 17, 1883, Hardy wrote the following memorandum: "Poem. We (human beings) have reached a degree of intelligence which Nature never contemplated when framing her laws, and for which she consequently has provided no satisfactions."[99] One's first reaction is that the idea (as contrasted with the tone or attitude it might suggest by way of metaphor) is far too cosmic to be of any human interest. Its generality is quite different from that of the idea of original sin, for instance, which may concern us daily and intimately and which we can test by an hour's introspection. We cannot do anything about this cosmic lack of foresight, however; we cannot be frightened by such desert places. The bare idea as such therefore promises little more than bare paraphrase, and we find this paraphrase at divers places in Hardy, notably in "The Mother Mourns":

—"I had not proposed me a Creature
(She soughed) so excelling
All else of my kingdom in compass
And brightness of brain

"As to read my defects with a god-glance,
Uncover each vestige
Of old inadvertence, annunciate
Each flaw and each stain!

. . . .

"Man's mountings of mindsight I checked not,
Till range of his vision
Now tops my intent, and find blemish
Throughout my domain."*

The poem continues in this manner for twelve more stanzas; it can do nothing but repeat its original proposition. The didactic idea, having no human or other context beyond itself to work in, cannot develop moral or dramatic interest. In the early "Her Dilemma" the same idea, introduced as though in casual afterthought, retains a generality of expression, but has both intensified and been intensified by a specific human situation. The abstract language there actually saves the poem.

In still other poems the idea and the human situation so interpenetrate as to leave no residue of unexplored didacticism. In *Tess of the D'Urbervilles* and *Jude the Obscure,* to turn at once to the novels, the original cosmic idea subsists as one of several dark undercurrents, but as a didactic formula is generally absorbed by a wide variety of human situations; it has become a meaningful pervasive judgment on society rather than a meaningless and isolated judgment on the cosmos. But the original formulation, irrepressible perhaps because of its bald and commonplace simplicity, now and again returns embarrassingly to the surface:

Vague and quaint imaginings had haunted Sue in the days when her intellect scintillated like a star, that the world resembled a stanza or melody composed in a dream; it was wonderfully excellent to the half-aroused intelligence, but hopelessly absurd at the full waking; that the First Cause worked automatically like a somnambulist, and not reflectively like a sage; *that at the framing of the terrestrial conditions there seemed never to have been contemplated such a development of emotional perceptiveness among the creatures subject*

---

*Thomas Hardy, *Collected Poems.* Copyright 1925 by The Macmillan Company.

to those conditions as that reached by thinking and educated humanity.[100]

Even this single sentence illustrates, though mildly, the progressive invasion of the moral by the didactic; the substitution of a formula for the humanly significant drama of Sue's darkening attitude; the encroachment of Hardy's static intellect on Sue's more fluid intellect. Our feelings about such a process vary according to the quality of the encroaching mind; the novels of Conrad and Thomas Mann become more rather than less distinguished as they approach abstraction and generality of statement. Much of the greatest poetry, including Hardy's, thus proceeds through fluid experience to finality of general statement; proceeds from the actual to the real. The Shakespearean sonnets and the best of the Shakespearean soliloquies are, I suppose, the most obvious touchstones for intellectual poetry of this kind: poetry which explores and animates the *lieu commun.* But though Hardy could think hard and intensively in verse, he could rarely do so in prose. He substituted obvious classification for thought:

She had begun as a poet of the Satanic school in a sweetened form; she was ending as a *pseudo*-utilitarian. Was there ever such a transmutation effected before by the action of a hard environment? . . . Yet Ethelberta's gradient had been regular: emotional poetry, light verse, romance as an object, romance as a means, thoughts of marriage as an aid to her pursuits, a vow to marry for the good of her family; in other words from soft and playful Romanticism to distorted Benthamism.[101]

Given an intellect which operates in prose at this level of conceptual simplicity and coldness, it becomes evident that the novels must transcend their theoretical conceptions before they can hope to interest us. Hardy was capable of intellectual prose of a high quality only when he frankly allowed attitude to dominate concept and looked at things "in a certain way." Thus we find in *The Woodlanders:*

Hardly anything could be more isolated or more self-contained than the lives of these two walking here in the lonely antelucan hour, when gray shades, material and mental, are so very gray. And yet, looked at in a certain way, their lonely courses formed no detached design at all, but were part of the pattern in the great web of human doings then weaving in both hemispheres, from the White Sea to Cape Horn.[102]

Thus the indifferently rational realist, who loved to classify and demonstrate, always threatened to suppress the dramatic, haunted, or nostalgic poet; the author of "The Mother Mourns" waited impatiently for the author of "A Trampwoman's Tragedy" to have done. Significantly *The Dynasts,* conceived in 1875 as a series of ballads, finally emerged as a sprawling historical panorama tied together by philosophical commentary. The theorist triumphed over the dramatist even more conspicuously in *The Well-Beloved,* serialized in 1892, which may be taken as an extreme example of Hardy's self-indulgence in this direction: a repetitious demonstration in seventy thousand words of the idea of Platonic love as vulgarly conceived. The sculptor Jocelyn Pierston is in love with an immortal essence, which he seeks to discover in a succession of "fleshly tabernacles." At the age of twenty he thinks he has found the "well-beloved" in the person of Avice Caro; at forty he pursues the fugitive essence in her daughter; at sixty in her granddaughter: "Each mournful emptied shape stands ever after like the nest of some beautiful bird from which the inhabitant has departed and left it to fill with snow." Pierston translates his dreams of the well-beloved into plaster and becomes a great sculptor. As an old man he is at last freed from the burden of his ideal longings, but simultaneously loses his artistic impulse and talent. He settles down to a calm and useful dotage.

The subtitle of this novel, "A Sketch of a Temperament," should have read, to judge by Hardy's letter to Swinburne, "A Sketch of the Artistic Temperament."[103] In the novel itself we find a summary of the sketch: "He was wretched all night. Yet he would not have stood where he did stand in the ranks of an imaginative profession if he had not been at the mercy of every succubus of fancy that can beset man. It was in his weakness as a citizen and a national unit that his strength lay as an artist."[104] This view of the artistic temperament, which is really a view of the so-called Shelleyan temperament, has been propounded by many sober professors of literature in the last half-century, but it is startling to see it advanced by a major poet and novelist. The dedicated spirit who cannot enter imaginatively into the lives of others, and who is therefore incapable of love, might have provided material for another short novel by Peacock; an incisive rather than merely tender irony might even have made palatable the succession of Avice Caros. Unfortunately Hardy looked on Jocelyn Pierston's immaturity as an artist's necessary defect; looked on it with professional sympathy. As a result the irony (which would have had some meaning if trained on Pierston's shortcomings as such) dwells on the mere fact of his repeated disappointments. Only in the second part—when Pierston takes the second Avice Caro to London as a servant, she the most commonplace of Galateas—does Hardy show any awareness of the human implications of his theme; this is the most interesting part of the novel. Elsewhere the "artistic temperament" floats in a vacuum, which is of course what Hardy meant it to do. We are not even told how Pierston worked, what kind of sculptor he was.

The book could have been saved by a genuinely critical irony, by the anatomizing of a familiar kind of immaturity. It could also have been saved by fantasy, by making of the Isle of Slingers an Arran Island, exempt from "Kimberlin" morality and logic. Hardy's preface tells us that he did in fact intend to present the island as some such fancy-ridden place and Pierston's Platonism as the natural endowment of an uprooted native son. Both irony and fantasy are constantly hampered, however, by the book's original and single idea: that Pierston is, and I quote literally, "the Wandering Jew of the love-world." It did not occur to Hardy, apparently, that imperviousness to change requires neither forty years to demonstrate nor a succession of identical experiences. Throughout the first and third parts of the novel he reiterates his formula constantly and at last wearily, turning it over and over without once pausing to examine it closely. Strong as Hardy's didactic impulse was, it seems to have consisted largely of an impulse to state and restate ideas, rather than to evaluate or explore them. It is small wonder then that a few reviewers (for reviewers must find something in a book to talk about) detected unmentionable moral atrocities. But the book's "immorality" is of a wholly different kind. *The Well-Beloved* is written in a simple and unmannered prose; it is not the worst book ever published by a major writer. But it is certainly one of the most trivial.[105]

We are confronted on nearly every page of *The Well-Beloved* by the original idea in all its naked simplicity; by the stark and undisguised outline. In other books Hardy's dramatic energy generally dominated his ideas about his characters, though it failed to dominate his ideas about ideas. But occasionally it failed even to rescue character. At a critical moment of *The Return of the Native,* and of Clym's fortunes, the author's outline rises abruptly to the surface:

> Three antagonistic growths had to be kept alive: his mother's trust in him, his plan for becoming a teacher, and Eustacia's happiness. His fervid nature could not afford to relinquish one of these, though two of the three were as many as he could hope to preserve.[106]

The occasional appearance of such barren summaries (there are a great many of them in *Far from the Madding Crowd*) cannot ruin a book or a character, however regrettable the momentary effect may be; at most, in Hardy, they reveal to us how a very plodding mind reasoned. It is more important to consider to what extent Hardy's theoretical conception of his characters conflicted with his intuitive understanding of them—or prevented any intuitive understanding and so crippled creative energy.

Some of Hardy's most impressive creations show no such conflict, since the original conceptions were both profound and energizing. Eustacia Vye is Queen of Night both in theory and fact; her private war with a "morally restrained universe" never seems gratuitous, as Felice Charmond's sometimes does. Similarly Gabriel Oak, Giles Winterborne, and Marty South are seen as well as understood as children of the soil. And Henchard so fully embodies the subconscious impulse to self-destruction, devotes his life to it so inflexibly, that the casual reader scarcely recognizes this very modern conception as such. As with Lord Jim, in some respects the same kind of person, a theory concerning human behavior dissolves into a whole life. At the other extreme, however, are the group of persons very obviously overpowered by the theoretical conceptions they are meant to embody; puppets dominated by their author's careful outlines. Little Father Time, compelled to symbolize a new generation's will-not-to-live, never transcends his symbolic function; he refuses to smile for historical reasons and kills the other children out of deference to a relentless Malthusian logic. Henry Knight and Angel Clare, as symbols of a new, half-emancipated, and already tired generation, are only slightly more successful, while Captain De Stancy, as exemplar of the exhausted aristocracy, is an insufferably verbose abstraction. Opinions differ widely as to whether Clym Yeobright survives his Tolystoian and Arnoldian principles; his bondage to Hardy's concept seems stronger to me than his bondage to Eustacia or Egdon Heath. Certainly Farmer Boldwood, clearly conceived as a victim of sex repression, goes through the necessary paces as stiffly and obediently as possible. From the moment he receives Bathsheba's valentine he acts out with inhuman consistency the inconsistencies of a distracted lover.

Most interesting of all, however, are the characters who resist and finally overcome their original formulations. Significantly these rebels against the author's outlines are nearly all women, though Jude as well as Tess survives Hardy's notions on heredity. Cytherea Graye, probably meant to illustrate a formal debate "between the dictates of her understanding and those of her heart," emerges as a charming Pamela and finally as the prototype of many Hardy heroines. Bathsheba, originally conceived as another Fancy Day—vain, fickle, and charming—becomes a massively self-reliant Diana. Did Hardy intend from the beginning that she should grow up in this fashion? In any event Ethelberta's change from the Deracinated Intellectual Female to a resourceful woman, determined to hold her family together at any cost, was almost certainly not contemplated. And Paula Power, coldly viewed at first as a symbol of the conflict between ancient and modern ideas, takes on much more human inconsistencies. Sue Bridehead's development from a symbol of modern restlessness and unfaith to a woman with harrowing sexual difficulties and at last to a victim of moral masochism is the most striking of all.

In each of these instances Hardy's sympathy, which was the great source of his creative energy, proved more powerful than his clearly defined intentions; his characters did not escape him, but they did escape his didactic view of their problems. In at least one instance, however, sympathy seems to have corrupted an energizing first conception, and the change is unmistakably for the worse. This occurs in *A Pair of Blue Eyes.* Elfride Swancourt appears fairly early in the novel as a minor Eustacia Vye, charmingly and naïvely vain—and capable of endless betrayal. She had first sharpened her feminine claws on Felix Jethway; a moment's innocent vanity had sped him to his grave. But Stephen Smith provides her capacities with their first serious exercise. She loves Smith well enough to go with him to London to be married, yet comes back to Endelstow unmarried, after seeing no more of London than the station. Here as elsewhere she is an "impulsive inconsequent," who seems incapable of telling the truth. She falls in love with Henry Knight but tells him nothing about Smith, who is biding his time in India. When the three meet for the first time, she cannot even bring herself to acknowledge that she had ever met Smith before. Thus through more than three hundred pages Hardy looks at Elfride with fascination and bitterness; this ambiguity of feeling gives to the characterization a brittle but very marked intensity. Eventually, however, Elfride is obliged to confess to the prudish Knight that she had been kissed and even engaged before; and at this point she suddenly wins her creator's sympathy. Hardy's indignation with Knight's prudery completely dissolves his critical and animating irony toward Elfride; her one fault, it now appears, was that of magnifying a minute mistake (the trip to London) into something too dreadful to be told. More sinned against than sinning, she becomes a merely pathetic figure and virtually disappears from the book.

Hardy should, of course, have revised the early portions of his novels to bring them into accord with his later and as a rule more interesting conceptions. Ethelberta the witty poetess does not develop into Ethelberta the family protector; she is a quite different person. Ideally, Hardy should have gone back and revised his first and unsatisfactory ideas about Ethelberta, but such care was hardly to be expected from a writer who turned from one serial to another. When he faced at last the task of establishing a definitive edition, Hardy found the mere improvement of phrasing a sufficient labor.[107] The critic must thus acknowledge with embarrassment that an undeniable formal defect, the inconsistency of characterization and attitude, was often compensated for by the fact that the unmotivated changes were changes for the better. We can only deplore

Hardy's rational realism, the didactic preliminary view he took of his characters, as a frequently crippling influence—and be thankful that he escaped it, even at the cost of formal unity.

Hardy was a realist, then, in his ploddingly responsible thinking about his characters and their dilemmas. He was a realist in other and more useful ways, however: most obviously in his ability to convince us that his dramas are true, that these things actually happen, if only in the pages of his books. This final probability has little to do with fidelity to fact, with the probability of science; "Christabel" is both probable and true in spite of the fact that women do not turn into snakes. The novelist creates rather than reflects life, and insofar as he is a great novelist he may establish his own scientific laws. In *A Pair of Blue Eyes* Elfride says to Knight, as she looks at the church tower, "Thou hast been my hope, and a strong tower for me against the enemy"; a moment later the church tower collapses. There is here a perfect fidelity to everyday science, since the restorers had been at work on the already weak tower. Yet the emotional context of the chapter does not permit the tower's fall, the grossly symbolic coincidence, and the reader is left unconvinced. In *Tess of the D'Urbervilles* the blood of Alec D'Urberville passes quickly through a ceiling, which is far more improbable materially, but in the context plausible enough. Mrs. Brooks's prosaic curiosity, its dull drabness in the face of an uncomprehended tragedy, would make convincing even some much more startling violation of scientific likelihood. What such an unimaginative woman sees must actually be there. So too *The Mayor of Casterbridge* convinces where it remains true to the laws of its own massive fatalism, to its formal foreshortening of the actual. Henchard's self-destructiveness, which is an undeniable scientific fact, makes plausible the furmity-woman's return to accuse him and the improbable coincidence that his own effigy should float by at precisely the moment he contemplates drowning himself. And the interview with the weather prophet, who has most improbably been expecting Henchard so far as to lay a supper plate for him, is as convincing as the interview between Saul and Samuel which it was meant to recall. Here Hardy is a realist in the sense that every great writer—whether naturalist, surrealist, symbolist, or mystic—is a realist. He has created his own universe so successfully that we cannot question its truth. In that universe, at its moments of highest realization, streams may flow upward or the sun stand still above Gibeon and the moon over Ajalon.

Most obviously, Hardy was a realist in his creation of plausible men and women—often very ordinary human beings, reacting to the extraordinary claims of life. This human truth, both general and detailed, is the foundation of his strength as a tragic poet and novelist, and also, since the truth is accompanied by sympathy, the reason for his great popular appeal. By contrast the source of Dostoevsky's strength, as well as Conrad's and Gide's, lies in re-creation of self, in the introspective plunge looked at with horror, in the invoked collaboration of demon and neurosis. When Gide attended the trial of a boy charged with arson, he speculated subtly on the possible sexual satisfactions which the setting of the fires gave. When Hardy attended a similar trial in 1884 he noted only the boy's manner of speaking to the Lord Chief Justice and the fact that the witnesses, who began their evidence in carefully prepared sentences, soon lost their control of language.[108] Hardy was a realistic observer of personality, feminine personality especially, and of character insofar as it betrays itself through personality, action, and speech. He also had a fine intuitive sense of what constitute, for simple unreflective human beings, the major "events" of life. This objective understanding of human dilemmas—and of the human dilemma—will concern us later. But it is well to recall now that even this kind of realism, this groundwork of human truth, appears in frankly anti-realistic art; a novel which totally lacks this human truth is a novel without interest. Even a devil and a witch must share our common humanity, as the witches and devils of Elizabethan drama do. Thus Hardy's stories of preternatural agency (such as *The Romantic Adventures of a Milkmaid,* "The Withered Arm," and "The Fiddler of the Reels") turn on the human emotions of ambition and jealousy, and even the "Mephistophelian visitants" show human inconsistencies. The realism of truth to human character is something quite different from truth to actual life. *The Mayor of Casterbridge* and *Jude the Obscure* are more selective than *Far from the Madding Crowd* and far more so than *The Hand of Ethelberta;* they deliberately exclude a great deal. Yet they also show a more comprehensive grasp of the human situation.

Hardy was also at times an orthodox realist, stubbornly faithful to fact, to the unheightened universe which we daily touch and see, to the unregenerated thing. He was alternately attracted to the occult and to the homely; as a consequence, his attitude toward literal realism was ambiguous. He wanted to be remembered, according to one of his late poems, as a man who had observed the minutiae of nature,[109] yet in 1919 he feared he had led the novel too far toward "postive realism."[110] No doubt he did encourage the weary realists of the 1920's, who described each minute process of rural life from the bearing of children to the shelling of peas, though the ultimate blame for this kind of fidelity must rest with Balzac and Zola. *Far from the Madding Crowd* at its best creates a pastoral world of antique simplicity, a fitting background for the changeless drama of love and betrayal, of faithful shepherds and glamorous faithless soldiers. At its least interesting it provides a detailed record of agricultural processes in Dorset in the seventh decade of the nineteenth century. Even the playful chapter devoted to sheepshearing at times anticipates the documentary and pedantic impulse of various American novels about the midwest. In the later novels, however, Hardy's descriptions of process tend to be symbolic rather than documentary: so in *Tess* the threshing of the wheat-rick, with its vicious struggle between man and machine, and the slaughter of the at last unprotected rats; and the pig-sticking in *Jude*.

Hardy kept his eye on the object. "Poacher's iron swingels. A strip of iron ran down three or four sides of the flail part, and the two flails were united by three or four links of chain, the keepers carrying cutlasses which would cut off the ordinary eel-skin hinge of a flail."[111] This entry in Hardy's notebook for December, 1884, suggests a concern for detail which could be both a weakness and a strength. His intimacy with the minutiae of rural life, even his precise knowledge of the legal status of the farmer and worker, helped him to see major human issues as his rustics would see them, for the material things which surround us inevitably color our feelings. But this intimacy could also lead at times to irrelevant word-painting. The one-time architect who pauses for formal and historical portraits of houses and churches is even more prominent than the countryman who looks at poacher's swingels: "In the corners of the court polygonal bays, whose surfaces were entirely occupied by buttresses and windows, broke into the squareness of the enclosure; and a far-projecting oriel."[112] To compose pictures (usually accompanied by the phrase "could be seen" and often by references to painters) was the most vicious technical mannerism of the age:

> Such a perfect, delicate, and necessary finish did the figure give to the dark pile of hills that it seemed to be the only obvious justification of their outline. Without it, there was the dome without the lantern; with it the architectural demands of the mass were satisfied. The scene was strangely homogeneous. The vale, the upland, the barrow, and the figure above it amounted only to unity. Looking at this or that member of the group was not observing a complete thing, but a fraction of a thing.[113]

This was the Hardy who could say of "the closing-line" of Eustacia's lips that it "formed, with almost geometric precision, the curve so well known in the arts of design as the cima-recta or ogee," but not the Hardy who could visualize a rustic's wife as "a long-legged slittering maid, hardly husband-high."[114]

Hardy has been praised by all his critics for the exactness of his countryman's eye; and justly so no doubt. He had a poet's as well as a countryman's love for things in themselves, and liked to enumerate their color, shape, and sound. This is realism in its original and purest form—an unreflective realism which at once leads to pedantry if indulged without restraint. Hardy's most memorable passages go far beyond the thing in itself, however, and the (perhaps) once visualized scene is transposed to a heightened and distorted impression of that scene, or even to an impression of the observer's mind. This impulse to reshape material things to a particular mood roused the normally lethargic stylist as no other impulse could. All the detached passages which follow—and all seem to me excellent—depend on a close observation of nature. The first, however, shows a greater love of words and images than of flowers, and many more such passages could ruin a chapter. The second, fortunately, shows more interest in the rhythm and movement of prose than in the sounds of trees. In each of the other passages the finely observed details subserve a general impression to be made. Here again the realist by native endowment was something more than a realist in his art:

Flossy catkins of the later kinds, fern-fronds like bishops' crosiers, the square-headed moschatel, the odd cuckoo-pint,—like an apoplectic saint in a niche of malachite,—clear white ladies'-smocks, the toothwort, approximating to human flesh, the enchanter's nightshade, and the black-petaled doleful-bells, were among the quainter objects of the vegetable world in and about Weatherbury at this teeming time.

To dwellers in a wood almost every species of tree has its voice as well as its feature. At the passing of the breeze the fir-trees sob and moan no less distinctly than they rock; the holly whistles as it battles with itself; the ash hisses amid its quiverings; the beech rustles while its flat boughs rise and fall.

The night had a haggard look, like a sick thing; and there came finally an utter expiration of air from the whole heaven in the form of a slow breeze, which might have been likened to a death. And now nothing was heard in the yard but the dull thuds of the beetle which drove in the spars, and the rustle of thatch in the intervals.

Skirting the pool she followed the path towards Rainbarrow, occasionally stumbling over twisted furze-roots, tufts of rushes, or oozing lumps of fleshy fungi, which at this season lay scattered about the heath like the rotten liver and lungs of some colossal animal.

Autumn drew shiveringly to its end. One day something seemed to be gone from the gardens; the tenderer leaves of vegetables had shrunk under the first smart frost, and hung like faded linen rags; then the forest leaves, which had been descending at leisure, descended in haste and in multitudes, and all the golden colors that had hung overhead were now crowded together in a degraded mass underfoot, where the fallen myriads got redder and hornier, and curled themselves up to rot.

There was now a distinct manifestation of morning in the air, and presently the bleared white visage of a sunless winter day emerged like a dead-born child.[115]

Read in this order, the passages might serve to illustrate the progressive domination of nature by temperament. Observation, in any event, becomes less and less particular.

As the historian of Wessex, Hardy wanted to be complete as well as minute. Here again his art survived a rather academic intention, which pursued more doggedly might have led to the triviality of a rural Jules Romains. Professor Weber designed an ingenious map for ten of the Wessex novels, showing that they seldom overlap geographically yet together cover the area from Oxford on the north to Portland and Bournemouth on the south; he also provided a useful time chart showing that the novels cover, here too with little overlapping, almost the entire nineteenth century.[116] Hardy further examined, unostentatiously as a rule, many of the ways in which a man could make a living in this area and during these years—from furze-cutting to the cutting of stone monuments, from preaching and trading to smuggling and witchcraft. We know that the general impression which the novels give of the agricultural worker's changing status was a false one; the worker's status improved through the period covered by the novels, but Hardy's pessimism darkened through the period of his writing them. But it is irrelevant to ask whether the overall picture is accurate, since a very real vanished world (though perhaps not a vanished Dorset) rises before our eyes. It is one of the paradoxes of criticism that it resents equally the use of actuality by contemporary writers and the distortion of actuality by writers who are dead. A writer cannot avoid using places and persons he knows, but if he is a writer of any talent he will not leave them the same. The blue peace of the Vale of Blackmoor and the lush green tableland of Froom Vale; cosy Mellstock, the leafy seclusion of the Hintocks and the open Weatherbury Farms; the treacherous hilltop fairs of Greenhill and Weydon-Priors and the gaudy urban insecurity of Budmouth Regis with its seaside promenade; ancient Christminster, Shaston, and Casterbridge with their monuments of Roman and later days and reached by the Roman roads; and Egdon Heath at the very heart of all, haggard microcosm of the wide yet imprisoning world—these are not to be found by tourists or in albums of the Hardy country. Hardy both observes and re-creates his world.

His considerable triumph was in the observation and re-creation of atmosphere, of the demanding spirit of place —a triumph which every critic has recognized. It is not so often recalled that this is an exceedingly perilous art, which was abused by nearly all the romantics and most flagrantly, no doubt, by Poe and by such popular novelists as d'Arlincourt. The extreme to which the abuse may be carried appears in Hardy's "A Tryst at an Ancient Earthwork" (*A Changed Man*), first published in the Detroit *Post* and consisting of seven or eight pages of gloomy and mysterious word-painting which introduces a trivial anecdote told in a few hundred words. But this was Hardy's one total failure in his prolonged effort to show human beings bound to the world on which they move, saved in fact by their very bondage to the soil and the living past. The Cornwall coast of *A Pair of Blue Eyes* and the rocky Isle of Slingers in *The Well-Beloved,* both intended to be regions of mystery where anything can happen, are partial failures which, like most partial failures, define the intention better than do conspicuous successes. Not climate and landscape alone or the trades practiced, but also the particular folk customs and traditions of a place determine the kind of human drama likely to occur there. Egdon Heath, visited by birds from every climate and region of the world, and so undulated that bonfires may be seen for miles, is preëminently a place where a man may lose his way following endlessly crisscrossing trails; where isolated human beings overlook each other longingly or hunt each other in the dark; where the human purpose is as minute and directionless as the purpose of scurrying ants which accidentally collide. *The Return of the Native* is a tragedy of universal and enormous cross-purpose; *The Woodlanders* is a tragedy of minute divagation from the norm. And thus the tiny Hintocks, where men depend for their living on trees which all but shut out the sun, is so secluded from the outside world and so tied to the visible past that even the slightest rebellion against tradition and the soil takes on a "Sophoclean grandeur." To succeed with symbolic environments as obvious as these required not merely genius but tact.

The idyll of Talbothays, which is certainly beyond praise, especially required tact. For the over-all intention could hardly have been a balder one: to blend Tess's recovery of calm and the resurgence of her "unexpended youth" with an environment which suggests more than any other both fertility and a changeless placidity—that of a great dairy. It is no exaggeration to say that Tess might have become, when subjected to such symbolism, a figure of bovine rather than natural simplicity. The further and tragic intention was to show her innocent and sensuous naturalism corrupted by Victorian nastiness; her purity, already violated by Alec's selfish egoism, must now be violated by prudery. What could have been more obvious than to import the half-emancipated son of a clergyman, the insufferable Angel Clare? To avoid an awkward and obvious symbolism here demanded a more careful building-up of the enfolding atmosphere than in any other of Hardy's novels.

It would require many pages to analyze Hardy's success in *Tess,* from the very first descent into "an ideal photosphere" and restoring calm, as Tess approaches the dairy, to the stagnation and "oozing fatness" of July. The dignity of the dairymaids at work is established at a single bold and explicit stroke, before the reader has a chance to form some less flattering impression.

Between the posts were ranged the milkers, each exhibiting herself at the present moment to the eye in the rear as a circle on two stalks, down the center of which a switch moved pendulum-wise; while the sun, lowering itself behind this patient row, threw their shadows accurately inwards upon the wall. There and thus it threw shadows of these obscure and unstudied figures every evening with as much care over each contour as if it had been the profile of a Court beauty on a palace wall; copied them as diligently as it had copied Olympian shapes on marble facades long ago, or the outlines of Alexander, Caesar, and the Pharaohs.[117]

Tess falls immediately and naturally into the dairy routine, which for the moment has been upset by the cows' refusal to give their usual amount of milk. The milkers discuss the effect on the cows of a new hand's arrival and sing a ballad to calm them. This ancient custom of the trade leads naturally to a tall tale of a bull quieted by William Dewy's fiddle, and to the legend of the cattle kneeling on Christmas Eve. In a very few pages Hardy thus creates the atmosphere of the dairy: the pleasantness of the milking, the good nature of the dairyhands, the customs and folk legends of the trade. And at this point Angel Clare makes his characteristic intruder's remark: "It's a curious story; it carries us back to medieval times, when faith was a living thing."

Thereafter every change in the relationship of Tess and Angel Clare proceeds naturally from some normal event in the life of a dairy, from some change in the summer climate, or from the telling of some tale which only a dairyman would tell. Clare first shows his interest in Tess, and they have their first conversation, after he ranges the cows in such a way as to give her the easy milkers. Falling in love, they need only wander a few yards off to be lost in an idealizing morning fog. And a story about butter that refused to come because a seducer was hiding in the churn recalls to Tess her own tragedy, which she had almost forgotten. The atmosphere of Talbothays, deliberately sustained over nearly a hundred pages, nowhere detaches itself from the human drama of Tess's reconstruction and Angel Clare's intrusion; nor does it ever submerge that drama. This atmosphere is a triumph of realistic art constructed from the simplest of everyday things. And like any triumph of art, it is something more than realism.

Tess of the D'Urbervilles and *The Woodlanders* are nevertheless Hardy's closest approaches to orthodox realism: to an impression of life as an unselective flow of plausible events. In *The Woodlanders* even the margin of chance is reduced almost to nothing as against the margin of error, and there are no grand foreshortenings of reality to correspond with Tess's sleep upon the sacrificial altar of Stonehenge. Perhaps the realism of *The Woodlanders*—its local color, its plausibility, its common-sense and explicit theorizing—accounts for its increased stature with critics of the 1920's and 1930's. Many of these critics found all the other Wessex novels to be essentially realistic too, perhaps because they could not conceive of good novels as anything else. Yet we now see that all these books are something more than realistic and that this something more is the source of their strength. In *Under the Greenwood Tree* it is a formal attitude, a deliberate and foreshortening playfulness; in *Far from the Madding Crowd* it is both a frank indulgence in the grotesque and macabre and an achieved impression of timelessness—as though these things were spoken and done in some remote yet changeless past. *The Mayor of Casterbridge,* so true in its psychology and even in its portrait of a town, is no more realistic than a Greek tragedy; it too is a vision and a seeming, distorted for the sake of greater truth. Even *Jude the Obscure,* for all its paraphernalia of naturalism, is a heightened and rigidly selected chronicle, the symbolic picture of an age. The "actuality" of the dying century was industrial progress, amelioration of the common man's lot, and a great deal of outspoken optimism. But the "reality" was sordid confusion and a heritage of spiritual isolation for not only the common man.

It is not merely in terms of our present taste that Hardy seems something very different from a realist. He himself was explicit enough about his intentions, though many of his critics refused to take him at his word. In 1881 he noted that the "real, if unavowed, purpose of fiction is to give pleasure by gratifying the love of the uncommon in human experience, mental or corporeal,"[118] and he went on to argue that the uncommonness must be in the events rather than the characters. In 1890 he took more definite stand:

Art is a disproportioning—(i.e. distorting, throwing out of proportion)—of realities, to show more clearly the features that matter in those realities, which, if merely copied or reported inventorially, might possibly be observed, but would more probably be overlooked. Hence "realism is not Art."[119]

The disproportioning, he had already explained in 1882, depended on the artist's temperament: "so in life the seer should watch that pattern among general things which his idiosyncrasy moves him to observe, and describe that alone."[120] Hardy was drawn by a strong natural piety to the everyday material world. But his "idiosyncrasy" led him to see and describe much beyond it: macabre ironies, visible absurdities, and unseen hostilities; witches, demons, ghosts.

Some of the greatest writers of the later nineteenth century saw demons and ghosts, but seldom the same demons and ghosts. *Anti-realist* is an embarrassingly comprehensive term, which may serve Huysmanns and Péladan as well as Melville; the term *symbolist* is scarcely more satisfactory and has the added disadvantage of referring also to particular literary groups. The anti-realists had this much in common: they found that the prevailing positivist complacency and bondage to hard fact threatened art or ethics or both. Beyond this it is very difficult to assimilate them under a single banner and intention. The complacency of Mrs. Grundy concerning the niceties of the British Sunday and the British home provoked one kind of reaction; the complacency of Taine, who systematically drove the occult into a corner, provoked a quite different one. How then can we group together Aubrey Beardsley's erotic reveries and Baudelaire's anguished Catholic efforts to prove the existence of evil? Flaubert was the greatest realist of the century; yet even he, hedged in by drabness, invoked madness some years before madness really threatened. Dostoevsky, who sought the devil in the subconscious, was an anti-realist. But so too was Melville, who tried to justify his inherited sense that the outer universe was divine or diabolic and in any event meaningful; and Poe, drunk with rhythms and words; and Dickens and Hardy in their different ways. And so too at the end of the century were Conrad and the young André Gide. Some anti-realists wanted to revitalize art, wanted to add something to the mirror in a country lane. Others wanted to revitalize ethics by finding a missing link of freedom in the inexorable chain of determined cause and effect. Not a few merely wanted to shock their betters. There is little in common between the anti-realism of Conrad and that of Wilde; nor could Hardy's anti-realism be farther removed from the anti-realism of the decadents.

Hardy's anti-realism was more popular and less metaphysical than that of his greatest contemporaries; he is one of the few anti-realists to whom the term *romantic* may at times be applied in other than a pejorative sense. Obviously he wanted to avoid the sterility of mere observation and Gradgrind common sense; he was an anti-realist on aesthetic grounds. But also he was a pure romantic, like Scott, appealing to the surprised child who lingers in us all; he was a popular teller of tales. The appearance of the Devil in the poetry and fiction of the last hundred years often signifies a skeptic's search for God. But Hardy, though he used the preternatural now and then, was very rarely concerned with damnation, with crime and guilt and remorse. His rare preternatural beings are there to puzzle and excite us, and because they have a time-honored place in the traditional ballad and tale. Significantly Conrad departs farthest from realism, in *The Secret Sharer,* to create a ghostly image of the divided and damning ego. Hardy departs farthest from realism, in *The Romantic Adventures of a Milkmaid,* to tell us a a fairy story. Nearly all the anti-realists were intensely subjective writers and were often markedly neurotic; Hardy as a novelist was neither. He was less serious than many of them, but also in some sense purer.

This is of course a relative judgment. For Hardy was also at times a genuine symbolist. His anti-realism added up to a distinct vision of things, however accidental or deliberate. Thus the extraordinary amount of lying and concealment in his books responds to the human fact that everyone has something to conceal. The large part given to chance and ironic mischance similarly responds to an actual absurdity in things: the discrepancy between the human longing for order and the disorder of daily circumstance. And to imagine macabre situations—that a secret lover should die in one's bedroom, for instance, and have to be dragged out secretly[121]—is to acknowledge that life frequently makes demands of us quite disproportionate to our strength. Finally, to suppose active hostilities—intruding preternatural hostilities, hostilities of physical nature, hostilities within the psyche—is to recognize the obvious fact that the world was not tailored to human measure. Hardy did not always think as explicitly as this and as a rule was commonplace when he did so. His anti-realism was more often the natural expression of a particular temperament (the "idiosyncrasy") and a great dramatic gift. A grotesque chapter may thus exhibit simultaneously the pessimist's disgust with the absurdity of things and the dramatist's delight in presenting that absurdity. A ferocious sense of fun may accompany a wholly genuine horror, in Hardy as in Dostoevsky or Kafka or Faulkner. The difference is that Hardy, unlike the others, seldom went "underground." He was startled rather than obsessed.

His closest anti-realist kinship is probably with Dickens, who no longer seems such an innocent figure of sweetness and light. But even here there are great differences. The world of Dickens is more consistently a dream world than Hardy's; nearly all his characters are sleep-walking automatons, and most of them are a little mad. Even the clerks who appear and disappear on a single page partake of the general insanity and are something more than natural. In Hardy's novels the dream world, with its nightmare conjunctions, impinges suddenly on an until then perfectly sane world of tradesmen, shepherds, and furze cutters; of everyday experiences and daylight desires. The unreal falls like a lash upon the prosaic and dull. In *Two on a Tower* Swithin St.Cleeve and Lady Constantine have a few minutes between trains at the junction to Warborne; to while away the time and say their goodbyes they wander into the gloom of the road outside. At this moment a phaeton speeds by, the horse jibs, and the driver's whip falls across Lady Constantine's face. The driver is Lady Constantine's brother Louis, returning from South America—the one man from whom she must conceal the fact that she has just been married. She manages to hide in the station. But the scar left by the whip requires that she take refuge for a few days in Swithin's cabin, where she leaves a telltale bracelet. The very grotesqueness of the episode makes it—whatever Hardy intended—something more than meaningless coincidence.

As an anti-realist Hardy comes closest to Dickens in the humors of his rustics (who never deviate from the particular roles assigned them) and in his occasional psychosomatic fantasies. But it is apparent at once that Dickens was far more interested in mania and hysteria than Hardy was; that he was fascinated by the isolated psychic oddity, the uncommon in itself. Hardy on the other hand was more interested in dramatic oddities, in the madness of circumstance. Is hallucination or coincidence the more interesting, psychic insight or cosmic irony? In *The Mayor of Casterbridge* Hardy hesitates momentarily, then frankly chooses irony. Henchard, in one of his darkest hours, meditates suicide. "If he could have summoned music to his aid, his existence might even now have been borne; for with Henchard music was of regal power. The merest trumpet or organ tone was enough to move him, *and high harmonies transubstantiated him.*"[122] He wanders out onto the moors, and does in fact hear "singular symphonies" from water playing at the weirs and hatches. He looks into the deepest weir-hole prior to jumping in and sees a stiff human body floating there. "Then he perceived with a sense of horror that it was *himself.*" Henchard, a deeply superstitious man, supposes this to be a divine warning; Hardy clearly implies that it is a hallucination resulting from the playing of the "singular symphonies" on an already troubled mind. But Henchard and Elizabeth-Jane, on returning to the weir, find that there is in fact something floating there: the clothed image which had been fashioned for the skimmity-ride and which had floated, by *a miracle of circumstance,* to just this spot. Macabre absurdity not macabre neurosis spins the plot.

Thus people are less astounding than the situations they find themselves in. However we rebel against these situations, we must recognize that they aroused Hardy's powers as a dramatist and stylist as nothing else could. Very occasionally psychic terrorism causes the appalling predicament; "Barbara of the House of Grebe" might have been written by Browning or Poe.* A legacy of hatred and the literal strictness of law, similarly, can provide adequate "cause" for the appalling: a chain of sinister logic leads to Jack Winter's execution for the trifling act of trying to recover his humiliatingly illiterate love letters.[123] But as a rule the macabre predicament is more nearly gratuitous. Hardy suggested the turn his imagination would take in the very first chapter of his first published novel. Cytherea Graye, attending a dramatic recitation at the Town Hall, glances idly out a window and sees her architect-father at

*Barbara marries Edmund Willowes, who is forthwith sent on an educative grand tour. He returns horribly disfigured as the result of a fire; seeing his wife's disgust, he leaves at once. Barbara marries Lord Uplandtowers, who surprises her in the act of kissing the statue of Willowes. Uplandtowers has the statue maimed to resemble Willowes after his disfigurement; he installs the statue at the foot of their bed. The first shock leads to an epileptic fit, but ultimately Barbara's terror perversely turns to love.

work on the neighboring church spire; a moment later she sees him test the strength of a scaffold pole, step back, slip, and reel off into the air. This was the first tentative essay of an imagination which would conceive far more harrowing situations: a clergyman obliged to read the funeral service over the remains of the father he had allowed to drown six months before; a bride of a few hours forced by her second husband to occupy a hotel room next to the room in which the body of her first husband still lies; a girl forced to clothe and manipulate the dead body of her uncle in such a way as to make him appear, to the steward looking in the window, to be signing the copyhold renewal; a woman forced to lay her withered arm against the neck of a man just executed, who is in fact her husband's illegitimate son; a duke forced to accompany his wife to an interview with the man he had murdered the night before, and murdered as he now knows without cause.[124] Some of these scenes appear in relatively slight short stories. Yet the same impulse to conceive grotesque or macabre predicaments produced some of the most memorable pages in the novels: Knight, Smith, and Elfride meeting in the Lady Luxellian's vault, Bathsheba opening Fanny Robin's coffin to discover her husband's illegitimate child, Henchard selling his wife and meeting the furmity-woman in court, Tess receiving Angel Clare in the boarding house in Sandbourne, Sue Bridehead hovering at the door of Phillotson's bedroom, Jude dying as the sounds of the Remembrance Day games drift in from the river, Arabella leaving him dead to go off to the boat races and to her flirtation with the obscene Vilbert.

Some of these major conjunctions were predictable, and character is indeed fate. But beyond them lies a wide area of brute chance and wholly unpredictable irony. Hardy's anti-realist use of sheer coincidence defines this cosmic absurdity, the weakness of human longing and planning in the face of senseless process. Hardy is not concerned with the gratuitous act, which proves that human nature is free, but with the gratuitous event, which proves that human nature is powerless for all its illusory freedom. The note slipped under the door that slips also under the carpet, the improperly sealed envelope that comes open in the hands of an enemy—these prove that no small part of chance has its origin in lack of foresight. But much that is called chance is properly so called and simply has no origin. A curate, having lost his love, departs for Boston and on the way over conducts a funeral for one of the ship's passengers. Years later, on returning home, he discovers that the dead person was his lost love, the first Duchess of Hamptonshire, who had wanted to be with him in America.[125] Christopher Julian, who loves Ethelberta, and Mr. Chickerel, Ethelberta's father, set out independently to stop her marriage; eventually, and though unknown to each other, they share a dogcart. Sol Chickerel sets out with the same purpose; in the dark his carriage crashes into the dogcart. The order-loving psyche wants its triumphs and its tragedies to depend on something more than chance convergences in the dark. But we are nearly always in the dark; the ways of chance are sufficiently inscrutable to warrant the supposition that purpose is at once blind and malign. This is what Hardy holds to, in his inverted faith, and it is almost certainly mistaken to suppose that his attitude toward Nature (or Fate) underwent any radical change. However his metaphors for it may change, he sees Nature as the enemy of mind: it is mechanism and senseless process.

Hardy's irony thus discovered both unreasoning chance and unreasonable predicament. But it often discovered them in a sense of fun. If we compare the collision in the dark in *The Hand of Ethelberta* with the collision of the lighter and the troopship in *Nostromo,* we turn from amusing inventiveness to moral imagination working at a very high intensity. Conrad rather than Hardy was the consistently metaphysical novelist, going beyond metaphor to a total and lonely unfaith. Hardy dramatized cosmic absurdity repeatedly, but often for the sake of metaphor.

There were occasions, nevertheless, when he showed a frankly metaphysical intention. The Cliff without a Name in *A Pair of Blue Eyes* provides the most Conradian of Hardy's pages, in style as in gravity of conception. Here the anti-realism significantly invokes both chance and predicament, and the particular predicament—the discovery of one's minute place in the geological scheme—is made to seem no less than the total human predicament.

The over-all irony, it should be recalled, has Knight clinging to the face of the cliff at the very hour that a ship passes within sight, bringing Stephen Smith home from India; the monstrously disloyal Elfride saves him by her response to "life-loyalties." Knight's first sense, after she has left for help, is that he is "in the presence of a personalized loneliness"; he sees his own plight in that of the tufts of grass and lichens clinging perilously to the face of the rock, against Nature's indifferent effort to destroy them. But that is a far too magnified view of things; he realizes, presently, that he is staring at something else:

an imbedded fossil, standing forth in low relief from the rock. It was a creature with eyes. The eyes, dead and turned to stone, were even now regarding him. It was one of the early crustaceans called Trilobites. Separated by millions of years in their lives, Knight and this underling seemed to have met in their death. It was the single instance within reach of his vision of anything that had ever been alive and had had a body to save, as he himself had now.

The creature represented but a low type of animal existence, for never in their vernal years had the plains indicated by those numberless slaty layers been traversed by an intelligence worthy of the name. Zoophytes, mollusca, shell-fish, were the highest developments of those ancient dates. The immense lapses of time each formation represented had known nothing of the dignity of man. They were grand times, but they were mean times too, and mean were their relics. He was to be with the small in his death. . .

Time closed up like a fan before him.[126]

And yet Knight clings to the cliff; he holds to his human existence against this appalling reminder of its minuteness. He still clings when rain begins to fall, not down but absurdly upward through a draft caused by the cliff's peculiar conformation: "It was a cosmic agency, active, lashing, eager for conquest: determination; not an insensate standing in the way." Like Martin Decoud, drifting on the absolute solitude of the Placid Gulf, he very quickly reaches the nihilism which cares nothing for life; Elfride returns just in time. The nihilism is induced not by the momentary illusion of cosmic hostility embodied in the lashing rain, but by the lonelier sense of a total and timeless indifference.

Conrad remains constant to his awareness of nature's indifference. The sea and the jungle may warp, test, or even symbolize human nature, but they are incapable of calculated malice. Their "malice" lies in their very lack of calculation and purpose; their seeming vindictiveness is a figment of our atavistic imagination, appalled by the unregenerate nature of things. Hardy would not content himself with Knight's nihilism, which resembled the nihilism of Conrad; he was determined to discover or create mystery, if only through metaphor and poetic faith, determined to spiritualize and humanize the natural world. To discover malice in seeming mechanism is no less anthropomorphic than to discover divine benevolence; either discovery is a protection against loneliness, and any violation of natural law provides comfort to the skeptical spirit. The desire to discover meanings behind the mere senseless revolution of things, even after faith has been lost, was by no means peculiar to the belated American Puritan. The famous chapters on Egdon Heath illustrate the fullest amount of mystery to be extracted from the merely natural—from the "nightly roll into darkness," from the suggestions of immense tracts of time, from the metaphorical equivalence with the mind's "wild regions of obscurity," from the physical conformations which make all human figures seem distorted and minute, and from the irregular trails on which all but the vigilant are lost. In other chapters, however, the mystery is more than natural. When Diggory Venn and Wildeve gamble on the heath, the natural mystery of the eternal and staring heathcroppers surrounds the unnatural mystery of Venn's luck with the dice—the game played to the light of thirteen glowworms. More obviously, the gargoyle which spouts water on Fanny Robin's grave and tears up the flowers planted by Troy raises natural logic to the level of preternatural irony and justice. To chance convergences in the dark, the symbolic instances of human perversity and cross-purpose, we must add those punishments and interventions by nature which occur more regularly than chance would allow; which violate natural law.

Hardy's anti-realism goes far beyond this, of course, and depends on the half-belief in spectres, witches, and the like. Elizabeth Endorfield in *Under a Greenwood Tree* is no witch at all, but a woman of sufficient common sense to be amused by her diabolic reputation. But Susan Nunsuch does believe in her own powers, and Eustacia does drown a few hours after Susan pricks and then melts her wax image. There is a great deal of such aesthetic half-belief in Hardy, which amounts to no more than a folk historian's love of local superstition and a dramatist's love of apposite symbol. In "The Withered Arm" *(Wessex Tales),* however, he demands and elicits a much greater suspension of disbelief. For Hardy did believe literally in the imagination's effective power over matter—in the power of the mind to effect bodily changes, in the telepathic fascinating power of the strong mind over the weak. Rhoda Brook dreams of throwing an incubus, the image of Gertrude Lodge, to the floor; at that very hour the mysterious withering of Gertrude's arm begins. Hardy suggests the possibility of coincidence—though he notes in his preface that the real Rhoda Brook threw off her incubus (with the same startling results) while asleep on a hot afternoon. But Conjuror Trendle, who could show Rhoda's image in an opaline mixture of water and egg, was aided by more than coincidence. Did his presence and reputation merely put Gertrude into a frame of mind in which she could materialize subconscious suspicions? This kind of question seems wholly irrelevant, for the powers of mind become no stranger thanks to a tumblerful of egg and water. Rhoda half believes that she is a witch and Gertrude half believes in the curative power of a dead man's touch, and they both experience a very prosaic disgust. But Hardy looks at their half-belief and disgust with fascination; he is too enthralled by the story, which he yet tells with great coolness and economy, to ask whether the story is true.

In "The Withered Arm" the historian of rural superstition blends with the speculative psychologist and at last with the storyteller, who believes what he creates. The ghost story and the fairy story operate at a different level; in them, the anti-realism is traditional, popular, and unspeculative. The ghost of Miss Aldclyffe in *Desperate Remedies* appears to Cytherea's "most probably dreaming" mind at a few minutes after four in the morning—the very moment of her death some miles away in Knapwater. The ghost of William Privett of Longpuddle is still more orthodox. On Old Midsummer Eve Privett is seen to enter the church and never come out again—although he has never left his bed at home. So do persons behave who are to die within the year. Three days later he does die while sleeping in Mr. Hardcome's meadow; at the moment of his death a white miller moth flies out of his mouth. At this moment too Philip Hookhorn sees William two miles away "looking very pale and odd"—hovering about the Longpuddle Spring where his only child had drowned some years before.[127] In "The Duke's Reappearance" *(A Changed Man)* the ghost of the Duke of Monmouth himself returns to recover the sword he had left in the keeping of Christopher Swetman, yeoman of King's Hintock village.

The Romantic Adventures of a Milkmaid seems to me frankly a fairy story; the Baron von Xanten's mesmeric powers are those of a preternatural demon lover. This short novel has caused Hardy's critics a great deal of distress. Since the majority of them could not conceive of Hardy's taking a more than archaeological interest in devils and lost souls, they were bound to misinterpret the story. It is, according to Professor Beach, "the most arrant pot-boiler that was ever turned out by tired and harassed writer of novels."[128] But the briefest summary shows that it is anything but grotesquely unreal realism. Margery Tucker comes upon the Baron early on a foggy morning and to all appearance saves him from committing suicide. He promises, in his gratitude, to satisfy any one wish she may make; her wish is to be taken to a ball. The Baron tells her to meet him at a distant crossroads (crossroads are the natural haunts of all other-worldly visitors) on the night of the ball. At first she sees no one, "but no sooner did Margery stand at the intersection of the roads than a slight crashing became audible, and her patron appeared." He directs her to a hollow tree, where she finds a lovely ball dress. A short walk, and they see "the brougham, the horses, the coachman, all as still as if they were growing on the spot, like the trees." Margery knows none of the fashionable dances, but she acquits herself well at the ball, thanks to the Baron's "magical and compulsory" power. Long before she has had her fill of dancing, however, he hustles her back to Chillington Wood where she must change back to the milkmaid before dawn. He insists on burning the ball dress and other finery, and before they separate makes her promise to come at his call. When she asks for some memento of their evening, he carves their initials, M. T. and X, on a tree. He says he does not use his Christian name.

The Baron's most characteristic act is to insist on the exact terms of the pact. This more than anything else suggests that he may be a preternatural figure rather than a conventional Byronic hero with strangely hypnotic eye. When he calls Margery on the day she was to have married

James Hayward, she answers humbly, "like an obedient familiar in the employ of some great enchanter." But the Baron, like the Geraldine of "Christabel" and certain demon lovers, does not want to do harm; he himself is under compulsion. He regrets that he has caused the marriage to be broken off:

"And, Margery, my last request to you is this: that if I send for you again, you do not come. Promise solemnly, my dear girl, that any such request shall be unheeded."

Her lips moved, but the promise was not articulated. "O, sir, I cannot promise!" she said at last.

"But you must; your salvation may depend on it!" he insisted almost sternly. "You don't know what I am."

He intervenes in her life on three further occasions, however: once to supply Hayward with the fine furniture Margery demands, once to see them married at what they suppose is his deathbed, and once (in an obviously phantom coach) to spirit her away—the coach and horses "black and daemonic against the slanting fires of the setting sun." Is the Baron torn for a last time between his impulse to take her to Hayward and his impulse to take her with him—as a companion among the damned? It is finally put up to her to decide; and, perhaps, to recognize his demonic nature. At the sight of his yacht riding at anchor, she "seemed to see all contingencies: she became white as a fleece, and a bewildered look came into her eyes." She wishes to be taken home. Did she not see, as one of the contingencies, that this kind of yacht *must* go to the bottom, after a few miles at sea? The Baron honorably returns her to Jim and disappears from Lower Wessex. "In his mystery let him remain; for a man, no less than a landscape, who awakens an interest under uncertain lights and touches of unfathomable shade, may cut but a poor figure in garish noontide shine."

To be sure, nearly everything in the story could be interpreted in other and realistic terms. And yet it is hard to understand why Hardy's critics failed to recognize that this was a story of the supernatural—or, at the least, that it was meant to carry supernatural overtones, that it was to be read and accepted as a popular ballad is read and accepted. For the Baron von Xanten was by no means the first of Hardy's invaders from an alien and perhaps nether world. Professor J. O. Bailey has recently taken a most interesting and valuable census of Hardy's "Mephistophelian visitants"; his article should go far to correct the preposterous academic notion that Hardy was a sober realist with occasional romantic fancies.[129] The "visitants" are intruders on Wessex simplicity whose appearance, name, and behavior carry Mephistophelian overtones, and who intervene at crucial moments to alter the direction of events—agents for good like Diggory Venn, or for evil like William Dare, but alike rich in "the subversive Mephistophelian endowment, brains." Professor Bailey's exhaustive article (which considers *The Dynasts* also) invites a few qualifications, as any attempt at completeness must. Most obviously, it is necessary to discriminate between the wholly human invaders, such as Newson and Farfrae, who disturb the action in a quite human way; the still wholly natural invaders who have Mephistophelian traits or reputations as do Mrs. Endorfield, Sergeant Troy, and Dr. Fitzpiers; and the invaders who are meant to be, or at the very least to suggest, preternatural beings—Diggory Venn, William Dare, the Baron von Xanten, and perhaps Wat Ollamoor. Newson, for instance, seems to have a sailorly rather than diabolic impulsiveness; Sergeant Troy a soldierly rather than diabolic glamor and a soldier's scarlet cloak. It is also necessary to distinguish between the fascinators (the mesmerists who attract and perhaps corrupt the innocent) and the spectators (inhumanly detached manipulators of tragedy, whose pleasure lies in "arranging" rather than enjoying life). Wat Ollamoor, whether diabolic visitant or skillfully hypnotic musician, seduces for sensual pleasure. But William Dare wishes merely to observe the aesthetic spectacle of the havoc he creates; he is figuratively if not literally impotent. The Baron von Xanten is a benevolent spectator by inclination and a fascinator despite his good intentions. Diggory Venn, according to Hardy's original plan, was to have remained a spectator throughout; "to have retained his isolated and weird character to the last, and to have disappeared from the heath, nobody knowing whither—Thomasin remaining a widow."[130] The circumstances of serial publication provoked the present and conventional ending.

Aeneas Manston of *Desperate Remedies,* rather than Elizabeth Endorfield, is the first of these occult visitants and a far truer adumbration of the later ones. He is also more obviously descended than any of the others from the mysterious stranger of popular fiction,[131] the tormented Byronic hero and the Gothic novel's fallen angel. Eventually the explanation that Manston is Miss Aldclyffe's illegitimate son dispels much of the mystery; so too William Dare's illegitimacy was to motivate in part his seemingly motiveless malignancy. In the later chapters Manston is alternately a damaged soul, longing to do right, and a very melodramatic stage villain. But his first important appearance is frankly preternatural, even to a "preternatural clearness" of complexion. He inveigles Cytherea into his house with the coöperation of thunder and lightning and stares proudly at the lightning without blinking; he has a mesmerist's compelling eye and can play the organ in such a way as to make a "poem" of the hypnotized listener's "own life and soul." He combines the pride and intellect of Lucifer with the softness of Pan. He seems

the last man in the world to put up with a position *because it seemed to be his destiny to do so; one who took upon himself to resist fate with the vindictive determination of a Theomachist.* Eyes and forehead both would have expressed keenness of intellect too severely to be pleasing, had their force not been counteracted by the lines and tone of the lips. These were full and luscious to a surprising degree, possessing a woman-like softness of curve, and a ruby redness so intense, as to testify to much susceptibility of heart where feminine beauty was concerned.[132]

Aeneas Manston is the most conventional and the least pretentious of Hardy's metaphysical visitants, but none of them should be taken too seriously. Dostoevsky's great ambition was to refute determinism through a positive definition of evil, through dramatizing the Life of a Great Sinner. He succeeded so far, with Stavrogin, as to make the Byronic hero a hero of metaphysical tragedy. Hardy no doubt felt the same longing to discern more than natural agency behind and in the senseless revolution of things; it was a characteristic longing of the age. But Hardy's use of preternatural suggestion shows none of Dostoevsky's seriousness of moral intention. William Dare is the only visitant who is truly diabolic in character as well as personality and origin, and his portrait is very incomplete. At most the others suggest Hardy's division of human beings into the strong and the weak rather than the good and the evil. The function of the strong—introspective, intellectual, constant in energy and purpose—is to make the weak suffer, whether they wish them to or not. The Mephistophelian visitant, whatever his conscious intention, cannot lead a simple, natural, and unreflective life. And it is to the simple and unreflective that Hardy's kingdom belongs.

Beyond this, Hardy's use of preternatural beings has no moral or psychological interest, and it would be a mistake to read into it the purpose of twentieth-century symbolists. Here more than elsewhere Hardy's anti-realism was aesthetic rather than metaphysical; a mysterious devil or demon lover could add color to the drabness of reality, could add the interest of the uncommon. The contemporary novelist may learn much from Hardy's half-successes and failures, but the critic is likely to find "The Fiddler of the Reels" Hardy's only unequivocal success in dramatizing the occult. It is to the other aspects of Hardy's anti-realism that we must return if we are to sum up his vision of things: to the grotesque and harrowing predicaments, to the vagaries of chance and coincidence, to the brooding myths of a hostile or indifferent universe. We may be grateful for Hardy's willingness to dramatize the supernatural in an age which recognized only the natural. But the natural is sufficiently strange, in Hardy's fiction at least. The homely pleasures of a country party may be disturbed at any moment by a knocking at the door of strangers who have wandered to it through the dark: a man condemned to death, the executioner appointed to take his life, and the brother of the condemned man.[133] It is against the background of such strange and chance wanderings, and in the startling conjunctions of the homely and the strange, that Hardy takes the measure of human beings—of their seeming minuteness and occasional tragic dignity.

OF MEN AND WOMEN

"HIS INTEREST IN MODERN SUBTILITIES OF emotion and of thought is an interest, which separates him, as a novelist, from the older novelists."[134] Thus Lionel Johnson could write of Hardy even before the publication of *Jude the Obscure,* his most modern book. The judgment is a startling reminder of the revolution which has occurred in our thinking since 1892. For today Hardy still seems a very gifted creator of personality, an occasionally gifted creator of character—and, as a rule, a singularly naïve analyst of "subtilities." These suggest three distinct approaches to the task of taking the human measure, and to them a fourth must be added: the moralist's definition of human nature in general terms. It is sometimes assumed that these are all subsumed under one process, characterization; that the novelist either possesses all these faculties at once, or possesses none of them. But this is manifestly wrong. The Johnson of Rasselas—totally unable to create life (that is, to convey personality) or to imagine fully rounded human beings and with no apparent realization of inner intricacies—yet showed a profound philosophical awareness of essential human nature. George Eliot was a massively gifted creator of understood and rounded *character;* Dickens was a superlative creator (not observer) of *personality;* Diderot, who could create personality but not character, and whose general understanding of human nature was exceedingly faulty, was a subtle analyst of the psyche and its complex anatomy. The very greatest novelist, to be sure, unostentatiously combines these abilities; he is at once analyst of the psyche, dramatist of personality, architect of character, and moralist of man's nature and destiny. Whether any such novelist exists is perhaps an academic question; if he does, Hardy does not belong in his company. He certainly does not belong, in any event, in the company of Stendhal and Dostoevsky, though both were incomplete moralists. The distinction may even be academic so far as relative judgment is concerned. To show that Conrad came closer to the ideal combination of analyst, dramatist, architect, and moralist will convince no reader who shares and strongly prefers Hardy's view of men and women. The distinction is nevertheless indispensable, for purposes of description. To dismiss Hardy as an analytic psychologist briefly is in no sense to question him as a creator of living personality. These are two entirely different things.

There is the further and always vexing problem of the historical estimate. Has the critic any right to expect Freudian subtleties from a novelist writing between 1868 and 1894? Has he any right to judge a writer according to categories of which that writer never heard or even to use those categories for purposes of description? These questions are not as unequivocal as they seem. The most obvious answer is that the essential human data do not change radically, and every neurosis antedates its professorial discovery. Even the civilization of the eighteenth century had its discontents, which often resembled ours; Rousseau, Diderot, and Sade observed them and wrote psychological novels which remain modern in many ways. Stendhal, Flaubert, and Dostoevsky (thanks in part to their own afflictions) intuitively understood and described complexities which modern analysts have only begun to explore thoroughly. And even Hardy, who probably had not read the few first theorists of this impulse, wrote one of the great studies of the subconcious impulse to self-destruction in *The Mayor of Casterbridge.* The novelist of the late nineteenth century must be read in terms of the Stendhals and Flauberts who anticipated so much of modern psychology, but also in terms of the more frequent and more "literary" psychologists (Scott, Hugo, Balzac, Dickens) who for dramatic purposes concentrated on monomania and on other extreme and often comic eccentricites. And the novelist of the late nineteenth century must also be read in terms of human behavior in any age. Do guilty or repressed persons talk connectedly and lucidly in their sleep? This is a question which the novelist can answer from his knowledge of guilty or repressed persons, from his knowledge of persons talking in their sleep—and from his sense of what is dramatically credible and useful. He requires no textbooks on guilt and repression. So too the critic, if he finds "negative hallucination" or the Oedipus complex in Shakespeare, is free to use these phrases—which refer to human states or situations and not merely to academic conceptions.

Intuitive understanding* thus operates, to some extent at least, independently of the contemporary state of knowledge; few modern novelists have improved on Diderot's portrait of the fragmented ego in *Le neveu de Rameau.* The dangers of a little knowledge become most evident when explicit analysis is attempted. The two passages which

---

*I use "intuitive understanding" in the sense given to it by psychologists when they speak of literary characterization. It refers to no less than all findings, conscious or subconscious, not based on formal experiment and analysis.

follow suggest how embarrassing the lack of an adequate vocabulary can be even to the richly intuitive mind:

The peculiarly bifold nature of Captain De Stancy, as shown in his conduct at different times, was something rare in life, and perhaps happily so. That mechanical admixture of black and white qualities without coalescence, on which the theory of men's characters was based by moral analysis before the rise of modern ethical schools, fictitious as it was in general application, would have almost hit off the truth as regards Captain De Stancy. . . It was this tendency to moral chequerwork which accounted for his varied bearings toward Dare.

There is an outer chamber of the brain in which thoughts unowned, unsolicited, and of noxious kind, are sometimes allowed to wander for a moment prior to being sent off whence they came. One of these thoughts sailed into Henchard's ken now.[135]

The greater compactness and interest of the second passage points no doubt to the fact that Hardy knew Henchard well and hardly knew De Stancy at all; the first sentence of this passage could nevertheless be taken for granted today. Miss Aldclyffe in *Desperate Remedies* offers a striking illustration of the conflict between reading, reflection, and intuitive understanding; the very marked confusion would hardly have been possible half a century later. On the one hand she is a Dickensian figure of illegitimate domination, tyrannically working on Cytherea's imagination; a less grotesque Miss Havisham, longing to revenge herself upon life. Hardy's first impression of her, colored no doubt by his reading of fiction, is distinctly unpleasant. But Miss Aldclyffe also has her "sweet dream," as we learn at the very end; she wants to arrange a marriage between her illegitimate son, Manston, and the daughter (Cytherea) of her one true lover, whom she had been forced to give up. Hardy's conscious intuitive understanding of Miss Aldclyffe thus reduces itself to two propositions, which are melodramatic rather than implausible: (1) a woman may be inexplicably attracted to a girl because she is the daughter of a former lover; (2) she may want to reënact her own unsuccessful romance, but successfully, by marrying her son to the daughter.[136] But intuitive understanding may be subconscious as well as conscious, and the "unpleasantness" which Hardy dramatizes is unmistakably that of Lesbian attachment.* At the first interview with Cytherea, Miss Aldclyffe thinks how nice it would be "to have a creature who could glide round my luxurious indolent body in that manner, and look at me in that way . . . and warrant how light her fingers are upon one's head and neck." On the very first night Miss Aldclyffe comes to Cytherea's bedroom, pleads to be admitted to her bed, flings her arms about her, and demands to be kissed more and more passionately. She soon asks Cytherea whether she has ever been kissed by a man. Her jealousy has nothing to do with the fact that Cytherea is the daughter of her former lover. It is a jealousy she had felt before:

"Well, were you?" said Miss Aldclyffe, rather sharply.
"Don't press me to tell—I can't—indeed, I won't, madam!"
Miss Aldclyffe removed her arms from Cytherea's neck. " 'Tis now with you as it is always with girls," she said, in jealous and gloomy accents. "You are not, after all, the innocent I took you for. No, no." She then changed her tone with fitful rapidity. "Cytherea, try to love me more than you love him—do. I love you more sincerely than any man can. Do, Cythie: don't let any man stand between us. O, I can't bear that!" She clasped Cytherea's neck again.
"I must love him now I have begun," replied the other.
"Must—yes—must," said the elder lady reproachfully. "Yes,

*Hardy was indignant over a relationship whose psychic discomforts he had imagined fully; in which he participated symbolically. The indignation got into the prose. But he did not know, perhaps, what the imagined relationship really signified. Later Miss Aldclyffe's feeling is explained as that of a frustrated woman for the daughter of her former lover (a highly inadequate explanation). Human neuroses existed and could be dramatized long before they were explained and "known." Or did Hardy know what he was writing about?

women are all alike. I thought I had at last found an artless woman who had not been sullied by a man's lips, and who had not practised or been practised upon by the arts which ruin all the truth and sweetness and goodness in us. Find a girl, if you can, whose mouth and ears have not been made a regular highway of by some man or another! . . . O Cytherea, can it be that you, too, are like the rest? . . . I—an old fool—have been sipping at your mouth as if it were honey, because I fancied no wasting lover knew the spot. But a minute ago, and you seemed to me like a fresh spring meadow—now you seem a dusty highway."[137]

The extreme frankness and clumsiness of this scene is the strongest evidence that Hardy had no idea what he was writing about, however unerringly the subconscious worked; there is nothing so appalling again before *Jude the Obscure,* and very little there. The prefatory note of 1896 is ambiguous: "As it happened that certain characteristics which provoked most discussion in my latest story were present in this my first—published in 1871, when there was no French name for them—it has seemed best to let them stand unaltered." This may refer to the "moral obliquity" in general, which Hardy regretted in his earlier preface of 1889—though by 1896 he was in a position to recognize a subconscious study of Lesbianism in precisely the way a later critic recognizes it. One passage in the novel itself bears directly on the problem of deliberateness. It is, presumably, innocent rather than ironic:

It was perceived by the servants of the house that some secret bond of connection existed between Miss Aldclyffe and her companion. But they were woman and woman, not woman and man, the facts were ethereal and refined, and so they could not be worked up into a taking story. Whether, as old critics disputed, a supernatural machinery be necessary to an epic or no, an ungodly machinery is decidedly necessary to a scandal.[138]

Hardy's conscious anatomizing, except in *The Mayor of Casterbridge* and *Jude the Obscure,* runs to far more spectacular divagations than those of Lesbian attachment: to psychosomatic fantasies, mesmerism and hysteria, epilepsy, the betrayal of repression or guilt through talking in one's sleep. He explores the middle ground between very exceptional oddities and fairly normal behavior only in occasional short stories. Both "Barbara of the House of Grebe" *(A Group of Noble Dames)* and "A Committee Man of the Terror" *(A Changed Man),* for instance, dramatize the fact that love may be founded on fear. "On the Western Circuit" elaborates a mild instance of sexual frustration and "A Tragedy of Two Ambitions" examines a very plausible crime. But many interesting hints in the early novels are left undeveloped. Very little is made of the suggestion that Wildeve could not bear to see pain or that Cytherea delighted to kiss the rod. In *Jude the Obscure,* on the other hand, hypersensitivity and moral masochism, explored at some length, go far toward explaining Jude and Sue. As a rule Hardy preferred more uncommon and more stagy disturbances than these. His psychological curiosity was melodramatic, the curiosity of a teller of tales.

Is "The Withered Arm" a study of rural superstition, the story of a remarkable coincidence—or a declaration of the imagination's real and astonishing power over the body? In the course of an analysis of Eustacia Vye, who fell in love with Wildeve because she wanted to fall in love, Hardy cannot refrain from referring to "the second Lord Lyttleton and other persons, who have dreamed that they were to die on a certain day, and by stress of morbid imagination have actually brought about that event." Mr. South identified his own life with the life of a tree, which he felt sure would kill him by falling on the house; when the tree was cut down he died from shock. Hardy's psychosomatic notions provide some of his most curious pages. The face is a true index of both character and blood, but this index is normally concealed by a stereotyped mask. Mr. Millborne and his unacknowledged daughter go for a row with the promising young curate; they get seasick and in their indisposition come to look "strangely, startlingly alike." The curate easily guesses their secret.[139] Elizabeth-Jane attributes her longing to look at the sea "to early marine associations," but Hardy adds that it was also due to the fact that "her blood was a sailor's." The day before she discovers that she is pregnant, Lady Constantine suffers hallucination; she thinks she sees a golden-haired child in a field. The quietness of the prose makes this one of the most successful of Hardy's psychosomatic fantasies—or, perhaps, intuitions.* Two of the most preposterous short stories—"Squire Petrick's Lady" and "An Imaginative Woman"—are also very impressive ones; they raise fantasy to the level of symbolism. In the first story a woman's frustration leads her to imagine that she has had an aristocratic lover, and that her child is his; in the second a lonely wife thinks so intensely on a beloved poet that her child is born with his features, not with her dull husband's.[140] "Squire Petrick's Lady" is a symbolic drama of the evil of class feeling; "An Imaginative Woman" is a symbolic and poignant study of loneliness. These are the real subjects of the stories, whatever Hardy's conscious intentions may have been; their symbolism ("generality," perhaps) is more interesting than their psychology.

---

*"It was evening, and she was coming as usual down through the sighing plantation, choosing her way between the ramparts of the camp towards the outlet giving upon the field, when suddenly in a dusky vista among the fir-trunks she saw, or thought she saw, a golden-haired, toddling child. The child moved a step or two, and vanished behind a tree. Lady Constantine, fearing it had lost its way, went quickly to the spot, searched, and called aloud. But no child could she perceive or hear anywhere around. She returned to where she had stood when first beholding it, and looked in the same direction, but nothing reappeared. The only object at all resembling a little boy or girl was the upper tuft of a bunch of fern, which had prematurely yellowed to about the colour of a fair child's hair, and waved occasionally in the breeze. This, however, did not sufficiently explain the phenomenon, and she returned to make inquiries . . .

The morning after the above-mentioned incident Lady Constantine, after meditating a while, arose with a strange personal conviction that bore curiously on the aforesaid hallucination. She realized a condition of things she had never anticipated" (*Two on a Tower*, pp. 386-387).

These curiosa have a certain value, then, as symbols or momentary diversions, if not as psychological intuitions. It is more difficult to justify the guilty or repressed persons in Hardy's novels who walk or talk in their sleep; they are either too sure-footed or too glib. Elfride slumbering on deck beside Knight moans and mutters at first, but finally betrays herself in compact and lucid sentences; the awakening Dr. Fitzpiers blurts out immediately the wrong woman's name. "What the Shepherd Saw" is as sombre and stylized as *Macbeth;* there is hence no need to doubt that the duke should walk in his sleep to the scene of his crime, twenty-two years after that crime, and there scratch at the earth like a badger. But the sleep-walking of Angel Clare is of course a major scar on the surface of a great book; it is so appallingly sentimental and melodramatic that the problem of plausibility is not worth raising. "He did not let her fall, but took advantage of the support of the handrail to imprint a kiss upon her lips—lips in the daytime scorned." The reiterated "Dead, dead, dead"; the perilous journey down the stairs; Tess's delighted acquiescence as she is carried across the narrow footbridge over the Froom and laid in the coffin; her fear that Clare will take cold; the return to the house, she now a barefoot angel leading Clare in woolen stockings—can we even be as charitable as George Moore and say that the whole might have been saved by having Clare crawl into the right bed?[141] Hardy's victims of extreme repression are as preposterous as his victims of extreme shock—and few novelists have distributed so gratuitously their internal hemorrhages and epileptic fits and undefined wastings-away. If Elfride's pulse can be raised to one hundred and fifty beats a minute by a defeat at chess, it is not surprising that Geraldine Allenville and Lady Constantine should die of apoplexy at the very moment of their triumphs.[142]

Hardy thus dealt amusingly with extreme psychic oddities, but floundered badly when he tried to dramatize familiar and very real neuroses. He has been commended for admitting the existence of sexual passion as early as *Desperate Remedies*. But the admission had been made even in England by Charles Reade and others. The treatment of Boldwood's frustration and clothes-fetishism is so extremely stagy that it seems to bc behind rather than ahead of its time. Captain De Stancy's suddenly aroused passion might have been imagined by the proverbial parson's-daughter novelist, and even Jude Fawley's erotic history is sadly incomplete. The great exception to the general failure in sexual psychology is the portrait of Sue Bridehead, which remains one of the most impressive in all fiction of a neurotic and sexually maladjusted woman—a living portrait rather than a case study, but with a case study's minute responsibility. Hardy's determination to tell the whole truth at last, and his overconfident assumption that the reading public had greatly matured since 1870 or 1880, are not sufficient to explain the startling advance over earlier novels. The fact that he had contemplated such a character for many years is much more important. "Sue is a type of woman which has always had an attraction for me, but the difficulty of drawing the type has kept me from attempting it till now."[143] Hardy could have said, more accurately, that he had never attempted a detailed portrait of the epicene woman as such. For "Diana was the goddess whom Bathsheba instinctively adored," and even Grace Melbury "had more of Artemis than of Aphrodite in her constitution." The sexual life of his early heroines was a subject on which Hardy had necessarily remained evasive. But how much of *their* evasiveness may not have had its origin in sexual repugnance: the inconsequence of Elfride, the fickleness of Fancy Day, the discretion of Anne Garland, the masculinity of Ethelberta? Sue Bridehead is perhaps a development from these earlier heroines, rather than a single and anomalous creation.

It is important to recall at once that Sue is not a Lesbian; there is no reason to quarrel with Hardy's own definition:

You are quite right; there is nothing perverted or depraved in Sue's nature. The abnormalism consists in disproportion, not in inversion, her sexual instinct being healthy as far as it goes, but unusually weak and fastidious. Her sensibilities remain painfully alert notwithstanding, as they do in nature with such women. One point illustrating this I could not dwell upon: that, though she has children, her intimacies with Jude have never been more than occasional, even when they were living together (I mention that they occupy separate rooms, except towards the end), and one of her reasons for fearing the marriage ceremony is that she fears it would be breaking faith with Jude to withhold herself at pleasure, or altogether, after it; though while uncontracted she feels at liberty to yield herself as seldom as she chooses.[144]

The omission of Jude and Sue's first years together (the years during which their children were born) raises again the book's most complex formal problem. The unbendingly realistic critic must deplore not merely the incompleteness of Sue's sexual history but also the passing over in a few lines of what must have been the only reasonably happy years in Jude's life. The answer to the second objection is that *Jude the Obscure* is not realism but tragedy and like all tragedy is symbolic; it is a vision of things and a reading of life, and according to that vision happiness is but an "occasional episode in a general drama of pain."[145] The novel formally and austerely selects only those incidents in Jude's life which are meaningful, which lead in fact to the most meaningful act of his life: his curse of the night when a man child was conceived. But even the first objection, the incompleteness of Sue's sexual history, is arguable. The few readers who do not understand after three hundred and fifty pages that Sue would be sexually reticent with any man are likely to have understood nothing in the book. In any event, the dramatic necessity to leave some aspects of character in shadow (not in ambiguity) might have demanded the omission. Otherwise the picture of Sue's adult sexual life is fairly full.

Sue combines, with her sexlessness and even repugnance to the "gross" sexual act, a very strong impulse to arouse sexual desire in men. She never outgrows her childhood oscillations between the tomboy and the coquette. She reënacts them with a Christminster undergraduate when she is eighteen and twenty, and later with Phillotson and Jude—and wrecks the nerves of all three. Jealousy prompts her to marry Phillotson and almost to marry Jude; she wants Jude to avoid Arabella not merely because sexuality is gross, but because she wants Jude to desire only herself. Her own happiness, as she half realizes at last, depends on reënactment of this pattern: to live with a man in an ostensibly sexless and fraternal intimacy, arouse his sexual desire, lead him on, reject him, and then do penance for the suffering she thus has caused. She marries Phillotson not merely to spite Jude but to punish herself for having made the schoolmaster suffer; she marries him a second time, when her self-punishing has become almost hysterical. Like all such persons, she *wants* to subject herself to punishment and horror; her religious and social scruples are the most transparent of disguises. But her horror of the sexual act is very real. The subject has been treated more extensively by twentieth-century novelists, but by none of them with more harrowing directness and economy.

Sexual maladjustment is not, to be sure, an isolated phenomenon like red hair or blue eyes; it is also, to use the jargon of the day, the product of psychic and social misemployment. Hardy saw this clearly enough and tried to relate Sue's sexual difficulties to the "disease of modern unrest." She was a pagan on theoretical grounds, not quite sure why she bought the statues of Venus and Apollo and turning automatically from Gibbon on Julian the Apostate to Swinburne on the pale Galilean. She was an "epicure in emotions" and a brilliant woman reduced to teaching children their ABC's and to fencing with the dull intellects of Phillotson and Jude. Hardy's effort to equate Sue's sexual disorders with the nervous disorders of the age nevertheless failed—perhaps because he conceived too sharp a contrast between the disoriented present and the calm stable past. Sue wanders among the various inadequacies of her own life, the experiences which cannot use her energies; but also rather too obviously between the dead world and the world waiting to be born. Her critiques of Christminster and of the Song of Solomon seem gratuitous, given her more fundamental isolation and difficulty. She is at her best when she frets against the Victorian atmospheres of her boardinghouse and of the Melchester Normal School, rather than when she doubts the authenticity of texts. Hardy's failure is nevertheless far more impressive than the obvious successes of his age. How many novelists in our own day have succeeded in dramatizing both isolated neurosis and neurosis as the product of social forces?

The origin of Sue's epicene reticence lies somewhere in her childhood, of which Hardy tells us almost nothing; the origin of her moral masochism lies there also. We are left, in fact, with two very slight clues: at the age of twelve she went in wading and was consciously, tauntingly immodest; and she was often smacked for her impertinence. Hardy variously attributes Sue's sense of guilt to an incomplete emancipation from orthodox religion, to the suffering she causes by refusing to give herself, and to the shock of her children's murder. But he nowhere attributes either the masochism or the sexual repugnance to childhood experience, as he would probably have done had he been born fifty years later. He was nevertheless distinctly ahead of his time in recognizing subconscious self-destruction at all, both here and in *The Mayor of Casterbridge,* and in understanding Sue's desire "to get back to the life of my infancy and its freedom." The self-punishing impulse first reveals itself sharply when she demands that Jude give her away in marriage and that they rehearse the ceremony without Phillotson. "Was Sue simply so perverse that she willfully gave herself and him pain for the odd and mournful luxury of practising long-suffering in her own person, and of being touched with tender pity for him at having made him practise it?" Later she feels obliged to tell Phillotson that Jude held her hand and thus humiliate the listener as well as herself. Her self-flagellation becomes intense after the death of the children, for which she feels responsible: "I cannot humiliate myself too much. I should like to prick myself all over with pins, and bleed out the badness that's in me!" She prostrates herself on the stone pavement of St. Silas' and feels "too worthless to mix with ordinary human beings." Eventually she forces herself to go back to Phillotson and does the final penance of demanding to share his bed. Her guilt works itself out in the very characteristic gesture of unnecessary housework. This, as André Gide was later to remark of his wife, is a typical feminine effort to destroy the hated self.

So summarized, Sue Bridehead may seem a monstrously unpleasant person, as unpleasant as most fictional neurotics. But she is, as it happens, one of Hardy's most appealing heroines; charming and alive from her first impulsive words to Jude waiting at the martyr's cross: "I am not going to meet you just there, for the first time in my life! Come farther on." It was difficult to make attractive such a stolid and passive sufferer as Tess; it must have been even more difficult to make Sue attractive in spite of her neurotic complexities. The survival can be explained partly by Hardy's success with dialogue and with characteristic gestures (the thumb on the parasol, removing Phillotson's arm, allowing Jude to hold her hand, etc.) and also no doubt by the starkness of her greatest sufferings. Most of all, Sue is alive not as a victim, but as a young and cheerful person immersed in daily existence, without ambition or vague dreams and with no pride beyond her feminine pride in the moment itself; a lover of outings and totally absorbed by whatever outing she happens to be on; her life naïvely and exclusively given over to the pursuit of happiness in a very gray world. She is haunted far more than most of Hardy's characters by the ghosts of guilt and the threats of future punishment. But she tries, more perhaps than any of his characters, to live in the immediate present. This is the clue to Hardy's sympathy toward Sue —and to much that seems indefinable in the appeal of his books. In very distinct contrast to Conrad, Hardy wanted people to be happy rather than good; he sympathized with their every effort to live and enjoy. He would have sympathized with the Rosie of *Cakes and Ale*.

What shall we say, then, of his characters who refuse to live, who stand obstinately outside life, who look in through lighted windows? The almost pathological unaggressiveness of so many of Hardy's men suggests an area of abnormal feeling dramatized without awareness of its abnormality—the unconscious study of a neurosis, perhaps unconscious autobiography. It would be more comfortable to ignore this curious fact, for to call attention to it is to draw down, no doubt, the wrath of nine-tenths of Hardy's older admirers and of all who still consider sexuality a minor and detachable element in the human composition. Furthermore, the historian can remind us that not merely Hardy's heroes but most heroes of the Victorian novel were strangely sexless; that sexlessness was the accepted fiction as well as the explicit ethical ideal of the age; and that Hardy was quite willing to present a moderately aggressive hero once he thought the censorship of prudery had become less severe. But the fact is that this sexlessness or unaggressiveness is more pronounced in Hardy's books than in those of his great contemporaries. It is not the absence of Judes which disturbs us in the early fiction but the rarity of fairly normal men such as Donald Farfrae.

Those who do seem normally aggressive, or of normal sexuality, are either grotesquely unreal in other respects, as is Captain De Stancy; or are broadly conceived as selfish rakes, as are Sergeant Troy, Wildeve, Bob Loveday, and

Dr. Fitzpiers; or as stage villains, as are Aeneas Manston and Alec D'Urberville. Most of the other men fall into the general category of the impotent spectator, who to a degree renounces normal life. Their seeming "impotence," it should be added at once, is something which can be observed quite apart from their explicit sexual history. It is a temperamental impotence, a lack of aggressive energy. In the absence of an adequate biography the critic must forego any serious attempt to explain the withdrawal and detachment of these men in terms of Hardy's own life. He can merely quote again Mrs. Hardy's own words for what they may be worth: "His immaturity . . . was greater than is common for his years, and it may be mentioned here that a clue to much of his life is afforded by his lateness of development in virility, while mentally precocious."[146]

The unaggressive, shy, detached spectator of life exemplifies in certain respects a high ethical ideal, and this no doubt is all that would have occurred to Hardy's early readers, had they wondered at all about the pallid reticence of his heroes. And yet, the unaggressive spectator of life has no little in common with the neurotic voyeur—with the man who cannot, because of organic impotence or emotional immaturity, enjoy normal sexual experience; who must get his sexual satisfaction from watching others make love, from watching others live.* All aggressiveness is to a degree sexual and at some point, however impossible it may be to locate this point, negativism becomes both abnormal and dangerous. William Dare, whose satisfactions are all symbolic and "cerebral," obviously suggests the impotent voyeur as well as the Mephistophelian visitant; the milder Lord Mountclere, who subscribes to fash-

*The neurotic voyeur may be a homosexual, an exhibitionist, an autoerotic masochist, or a paedophile—and no doubt other things. Perhaps most characteristically he shows the sadism of Faulkner's Popeye and commits rape vicariously or symbolically. Hardy's pallid spectators are not Popeyes.

ion books and plates for their drawings of women and takes Lord Steyne's cynical pleasure in observing female audacity, shows to some degree the same temperament. These characters are undisguisedly vicious, and here at least there need be no reluctance to call a spectator a voyeur. The psychologist would insist, however, that all those whose satisfactions are symbolic and imaginative rather than actual, from Diggory Venn to Jocelyn Pierston, belong to the same general type; that these characters too are abnormal, however innocent or kindly their intentions. The psychologist must also add up his clues, remembering that "innocent" clues are generally the most revealing ones. The amount of actual "peeping" in Hardy's novels—of lingering about to catch a furtive glimpse of the beloved as she passes her window, etc.—is too considerable to be ignored. Such peeping occurs in every novel; even the Bishop of Melchester peeps.[147] It goes without saying that little of this peeping is salacious, as it is with Captain De Stancy,[148] and that a great deal of it may have been provoked by the necessities of plot. What it chiefly suggests, however, is a vision of an unaggressive tendency to live in the imagination only and a long preoccupation with lonely withdrawal. The most obvious spectator in Hardy's fiction is not Captain De Stancy or the benevolent Diggory Venn but Jocelyn Pierston—who rents a house from which he can watch every move of the second Avice Caro! He "felt in no hurry to obtrude his presence just now"; to observe her was the "real business of his sojourn."[149] He is, as a young man of twenty or as a young man of sixty, incapable of a normal human relationship; the sexual as well as the moral drama occurs entirely within his mind. *The Well-Beloved,* which defines the artist as a Platonist, could also be said to define the artist as a voyeur —a definition which has its measure of truth. For though art is not founded on insanity, it is founded at least in part on some maladjustment to life. The perfectly adjusted person, could we conceive of him, would have no symbolic life at all. It does not discredit the contemplative ascetic or the saint obsessed with suffering or the self-immolating artist to say that he has both exploited and survived his deficiencies—and that these deficiencies may have been sexual. The criminal voyeur such as William Dare and the nobly self-renouncing Diggory Venn may have more in common than we like to think.

The ethical problem, however, concerns the ways in which these two types differ. Here some of Hardy's critics have misunderstood him so far as to confuse the self-sacrificing purity of the symbolic Diggory Venn, of the generous and conventional Giles Winterborne, and of the nasty Angel Clare. These men have nothing more in common than their lack of masculine aggressiveness. The indestructible Gabriel Oak is the one unaggressive hero who is frankly idealized, unless we ignore Hardy's own description of Venn. He is, in fact, as different as possible from the egoist Jocelyn Pierston:

> What a way Oak had, she thought, of enduring things. Boldwood, who seemed so much deeper and higher and stronger in feeling than Gabriel, had not yet learnt, any more than she herself, the simple lesson which Oak showed a mastery of by every turn and look he gave—that among the multitude of interests by which he was surrounded, those which affected his personal well-being were not the most absorbing and important in his eyes. Oak meditatively looked upon the horizon of circumstances without any special regard to his own standpoint in the midst.[150]

Hardy admired Oak's unselfishness, yet knew that even such unselfishness as this could cause unhappiness. Bathsheba "could not really forgive him for letting his wish to marry her be eclipsed by his wish to do her good."[151] Conrad in *Chance* and Gide in *La Porte étroite* recognized that generous self-denial can cause as much mischief as egoism; Hardy recognized this too.* The "heroic" Egbert

---

*Compare the suffering caused by Gertrude Stein's Jeff Campbell (*Melanctha*), to take an example from frankly "psychologizing" fiction.

Mayne is an adumbration of John Loveday and Giles Winterborne; his generosity infuriates:

> There were two things to be thought of, the saving of her dignity, and the saving of his or her happiness. That to accomplish the first he ought voluntarily to leave the village before their attachment got known, and never seek her again, was what he sometimes felt; but the idea brought such misery along with it that it died out under contemplation.
>
> He determined at all events to put the case clearly before her, to heroically set forth at their next meeting the true bearings of their position, which she plainly did not realise to the full as yet. . . Yes, it was his duty to warn her, even though by so doing he would be heaping coals of fire on his own head. For by acting upon his hint she would be lost to him. . .
>
> She was quite hurt at being treated with justice, and a crowd of tears came into her sorrowful eyes. She had never thought of half that he feared, and almost questioned his kindness in enlightening her.[152]

As a lover John Loveday of *The Trumpet-Major* would take no unfair advantage even of the drunken Festus Derriman; Anne Garland was no doubt well advised to prefer his more selfish but also more masculine brother. A little aggressiveness on Giles Winterborne's part would have saved Grace Melbury as well as himself a great deal of suffering. "But he continued motionless and silent in that gloomy Niflheim or fogland which involved him, and she proceeded on her way." "Move another step towards her he would not. He would even repulse her—*as a tribute to conscience.*" The exasperated Grace says what nearly all of Hardy's heroines might have said: "If you had only shown half the boldness before I married that you show now, you would have carried me off for your own, first instead of second."[153] Hardy looks on Giles's final and grotesque "heroism," his willingness to die from exposure rather than endanger Grace's reputation, with mingled sympathy and horror. Giles was a simple son of the soil.

But he was not, any more than the Reverend Cope, a "passionate lover of the old-fashioned sort."

For this is the point that has generally been overlooked. Hardy constructed an ethic of fidelity and generous simplicity, but not an ethic of rejection. He identified himself to a degree with his sexless and self-denying heroes and so could not withhold imaginative sympathy. But he also criticized their habit of renunciation, their immature refusal to accept life and enjoy it. Thus his ambiguities and moral hesitations are not unlike those of Henry James. His ideal of character is clear enough—that of a faithful and generous extrovert who is also a "passionate lover of the old-fashioned sort," who knows when to sacrifice his own claims but also when to advance them, who does not stand shyly outside the active current of life. But he found it nearly impossible to dramatize such a person; only the coldly conceived Donald Farfrae even approaches the formula. He was much more at home with Christopher Julian and his "habit of dreaming instead of doing" than with "the active, the rapid, the people of splendid momentum." He was more at home with Diggory Venn, who "had relinquished his proper station in life for want of interest in it" and who could not escape "the old track of manoeuvring on Thomasin's account."[154] The original ending of *The Return of the Native* would have been more satisfactory even for Diggory, who was certainly the kind of man to prefer Thomasin's lost glove to Thomasin herself. The real drama of life could play itself only in the detached and brooding mind. Edward Springrove, Stephen Smith, Egbert Mayne, Christopher Julian, George Somerset—all are curiously passive and colorless; as colorless in personality as Hardy himself seemed to nearly everyone who met him casually. They drift as sleepwalkers through scenes in which other men, and women particularly, love and hate with passion—strive, struggle, and enjoy. They do not as a rule criticize this turbulence prudishly; they look on it rather with envy. But it is not for them to participate. Their pleasure must come from the meditative looking on.

The men are paralyzed less by introspection than by this lack of normal aggressiveness, by an at least figurative lack of virility. Hardy saw this clearly enough, though no doubt he did not always or even often think of it in sexual terms. These men seemed to him, as did Clym Yeobright in particular, "the modern man—the type to which the great mass of educated modern men of ordinary capacity are assimilating more or less."[155] Henry Knight and Angel Clare really belong to the same type, but Hardy criticizes them much more sharply. He seems conscious, in dealing with them, of defects which the others also show. Henry Knight (with whom Hardy appears to have identified himself more than with Stephen Smith) was "not shaped by Nature for a marrying man. Perhaps his lifelong constraint toward women, which he had attributed to accident, was not chance after all, but the natural result of instinctive acts so minute as to be undiscernible even by himself."[156] Elsewhere Hardy attributes Knight's immaturity (his desire to be Elfride's first lover) to an imagination "fed up to preternatural size by lonely study and silent observations of his kind," to emotions "drawn out long and delicate" by seclusion.[157] With Angel Clare, who shows the same immaturity, Hardy's criticism becomes specific and on the whole unambiguous. Clare exhibits both the "self-combatting proclivity of the supersensitive" and Jocelyn Pierston's "will to subdue the grosser emotion to the subtler emotion, the substance to the conception, the flesh to the spirit."[158]

Some might risk the old paradox that with more animalism he would have been the nobler man. We do not say it. Yet Clare's love was ethereal to a fault, imaginative to impracticability. *With these natures corporeal presence is sometimes less appealing than corporeal absence: the latter creating an ideal presence that conveniently drops the defects of the real.* She found that her personality did not plead her cause so forcibly as she had anticipated. The figurative phase was true: she was another woman than the one who had excited his desire.[159]

The passage shows a great deal of intuitive and moral understanding. If we look back not merely on Henry Knight but on Edward Springrove and his colorless descendents, we see that Hardy had come far closer to understanding the inadequacy of his unaggressive heroes; criticism now far outweighed sympathy. The portrait of Jocelyn Pierston shows a rather startling return of sympathy; this is perhaps explained by the fact that *The Well-Beloved* had been planned much earlier. Or did Hardy hold to the end to his tenuous distinctions between the shy rustic who is naturally generous and unaggressive, the "modern man" who has lost his will to live, the lonely intellectual who lives only in his dreams, and the egotistical artist who is necessarily incapable of normal enjoyment? None of the four, and no character in Hardy, shows the disgust for normal sexual experience which may be discerned in certain characters of Conrad and Gide. They all betray, rather, an unmistakable if only spiritual impotence, and they cause others to suffer as a result. The future biographer will have to decide what relationship this has to Hardy's own personal history. It is entirely possible that this personal history underwent certain important changes even after Hardy began to write fiction. "He himself said humorously in later times that he was a child till he was sixteen, a youth till he was twenty-five, and a young man till he was nearly fifty."[160] Some novelists, however much they change personally, can dramatize subjectively only their earlier selves.

For the present the critic is reduced to conjecture so obscure as to remain valueless. He can merely point to the fact that Hardy's men, prior to *The Mayor of Casterbridge*, are inadequate as human beings and even more inadequate as fictional creations. Hardy's great gift for conveying living personality reveals itself rather in his portraits of rustics and of women. It is perhaps significant that the women in particular are seen as objects—fascinating, incomprehensible, strange.

The rustics must of course be distinguished from the "country folk" and the changeful or suffering characters who, like Gabriel Oak, Giles Winterborne, and Marty South, are actively involved in the dramas. The true Hardy rustic is of *personality* all compact: of gestures, turns of phrase, humors, and deformities. He has a past history, which he delights to relate, but no present history and conflict. For he is immune to suffering and change; he is part of the landscape, and his stability is a fixed screen for the rebellious and changeful protagonists. The rustics of Scott are personalities who threaten to become characters and very often do; the "originals" of Dickens are obsessed madmen walking on a leash of daily habit; the rustics of Shakespeare are cheerful wanderers in an idyllic dream. The conflict of personality and character (which we discover in Elfride Swancourt and Fancy Day—and in Falstaff, to use the radical example) seldom occurs in Hardy's rustics, who remain formal, attitudinizing, and childlike. Though they enunciate the stable moralities against which rural divergence and delinquency may be measured, they themselves are quite unmoral. They are not, that is, obliged to make decisions as real human beings are. They drift from the farm to the church to the inn, changeless and indestructible, timelessly detached from the tragedies on which they comment so pungently. The unmarriageable Christian Cantle must reduce all experience to his own unmarriageable thinness and timidity; the shy Joseph Poorgrass must see everything in terms of his tendency to blush. The rustics are very much alive, but they are not real human beings, shuffled and hedged in by circumstance. It is curious that this should be so.

For they are the backbone of the community in and about Weatherbury and Egdon. They have always been there and will seemingly survive all catastrophe. Yet they are unmistakeably brittle, decorative, fictitious, *literary*—as literary as Dogberry and Bottom.

The rustics appear in their undisguised artificiality only in *Far from the Madding Crowd* and *The Return of the Native*. We must find some other name for the more real and perhaps less interesting villagers and agricultural laborers portrayed in the later novels. Their simplicity is idealized in *The Woodlanders* and their generosity in *Tess*. But in *Jude the Obscure* the simplicity has become mere dullness of wit, and the generosity has disappeared in a harsh and cynical realism. The Mellstock villagers of *Under the Greenwood Tree,* who seem to have been based on actual remembered persons, stand somewhere between reality and convention. But the truest and most famous of the rustics—Billy Smallbury, Jan Coggan, Joseph Poorgrass, Grandfer and Christian Cantle, Timothy Fairway, *et al.*—are largely conventional; it would be both unjust and absurd to examine them as real human beings, to examine for instance their motives. "To make men moral something more is requisite than to turn them out to grass," George Eliot observed. The rustics of *Far from the Madding Crowd* and *The Return of the Native* provide a certain amount of comic relief; they also provide a formal chorus of limited but assured wisdom. And they provide, with their rambling tales and memories, a firm connection with the past. But they do not provide "rural realism." They are not Dorset workfolk of the nineteenth century, but relics of Wessex's still living past. The few critics who have taken them to be actual Dorset workfolk of the nineteenth century, faithfully observed and chronicled, could have been spared this most radical mistake by a merest surview of the poems, especially of *Time's Laughingstocks.*

For it is in the poems that we see the rustics as human beings—trapped in difficult human situations; having changeful and significant inner lives; corrupt and perverse at times, as well as tolerant and enduring; humanly bereft of their coy and childlike innocence. "A Trampwoman's Tragedy" is a stark and compact tale of rustic jealousy, perversity, and murder; "A Sunday Morning Tragedy," of abortion and death; "Julie-Jane," of mere promiscuity; "The Dark-Eyed Gentlemen" and many other poems, of seduction. The rustics of the poems escape, often entirely, the patronizing and Dickensian tenderness of the novels; they are permitted complicated dreams, desires, and disappointments—permitted in a word maturity. At most, as in "She Hears the Storm" and "At Casterbridge Fair," they are subjected to the bitter, slight, and detached tenderness of an A. E. Housman. More often they are allowed the direct hard choices and emotional intensities which, in the novels, are reserved for persons of a slightly higher social standing. The country folk of the poems are the actors, not the spectators, of tragedy; they are human beings, not amusing pets. It is to them, and to the Giles and the Marty Souths, that we must look for Hardy's realism of country life.

This being so, the conventional rustics offer admirable examples of the creation of living personality as opposed to the creation of living character. Hardy's critics have done these rustics full justice and even a little more than justice; there is hence no need to analyze their success at length. The material was certainly energizing, though it is hard to say why. The methods—easily discernible if one examines the chapters on the rustics directly instead of awaiting their appearance in the full context of the novels—are in fact very rudimentary. A great deal is made of embarrassed fixed stares, of agonized clearings of the throat, of shy shufflings of the feet; a great deal is made also of such details as Jacob's one tooth—"in the left centre of his upper jaw, which made much of itself by standing prominent, like a millstone in a bank." An affectionate pseudo realism dwells repeatedly on the rustics' indelicacy and on their indifference to good "clane dirt." Mrs. Dewy, being a social climber, wonders how she ever allowed herself to marry into a family of "sich vulgar sweaters" and cannot accept her husband's poor excuse: "If I be hot week-days, I must be hot Sundays." But Gabriel Oak, though no ordinary rustic, never fusses about "dirt in its pure state":

"And here's a mouthful of bread and bacon that mis'ess have sent, shepherd. The cider will go down better with a bit of victuals. Don't ye chaw quite close, shepherd, for I let the bacon fall in the road outside as I was bringing it along, and may be 'tis rather gritty. There, 'tis clane dirt; and all know what that is, as you say, and you bain't a particular man we see, shepherd."

"True, true—not at all," said the friendly Oak.

"Don't let your teeth quite meet, and you won't feel the sandiness at all. Ah! 'tis wonderful what can be done by contrivance!"[161]

Self-depreciation—frank, obstinate, humorous, and sometimes proud—is the great distinguishing characteristic of Hardy's rustics, as it is of many of Dickens' workingmen. Clerk Crickett of *Desperate Remedies* is the first of many to boast of what others would conceal about their wives. Not only the whole Mellstock choir but Thomas Leaf himself takes pride in Leaf's feeble-mindedness. The barmaid Maryann, who asks if anyone knows "of a crooked man" for her "or a lame, or any second-hand fellow at all," has a kind of modest charm, but the ancient maltster is anything but modest about his extreme weakness and old age:

A strange old piece, ye say! . . . At the same time ye be no old man worth naming—no old man at all. Yer teeth baint half gone yet; and what's an old man's standing if so be his teeth baint gone? Weren't I stale in wedlock afore ye were out of arms? 'Tis a poor thing to be sixty, when there's people far past four-score—a boast weak as water.[162]

It is a rare rustic who tries to cure his own deficiencies, though the blushing Joseph Poorgrass once went so far as to take a job as errand man at the Woman's Skittle Alley in Casterbridge. " 'Twas a horrible evil situation, and a very curious place for a good man."

The deficiencies and humors are the individual's function and interest in life. "I've asked 'em," Christian Cantle replies, when asked how he knows the women won't have him.

"Sure I should never have thought you had the face. Well, and what did the last one say to ye? Nothing that can't be got over, perhaps, after all?"

" 'Get out of my sight, you slack-twisted, slim-looking fool,' was the woman's words to me."

"Not encouraging, I own," said Fairway. " 'Get out of my sight, you slack-twisted, slim-looking fool,' is rather a hard way of saying No. But even that might be overcome by time and patience, so as to let a few grey hairs show themselves in the hussy's head. How old be you, Christian?"

"Thirty-one last tatie-digging, Mister Fairway."[163]

All this has its real charm and brilliance but can become very tiresome. The constables who skulk in a Casterbridge alley rather than try to stop the skimmity-ride, and who prudently hide their staves in a waterpipe, are true descendants of Falstaff's poltroonish soldiers. And if Abel Whittle's device for getting to work on time (to tie to his great toe a string, which he hangs out the window for his friends to pull) is worthy of Boccaccio and Dickens, Henchard's punishment (to drive Whittle to work without breeches) is as worthy of Smollett. But this dramatic use of caricature is comparatively rare. The rustics come to life most notably through their gnomic and metaphorical speeches on human destiny—and on the particular obscure destinies around them. From first to last Hardy was able to *create* (not reproduce) the speaking accents of quick, shrewd, and often pitilessly critical minds. So we hear Clerk Crickett on Cytherea Graye and Nance Mockridge and Mother Cuxsom on Michael Henchard:

"Stylish accountrements about the head and shoulders," said the clerk. "Sheenen curls, and plenty o 'em."

"Well—there's a difference between 'em, though he do call himself a teetotaller," said Nancy Mockridge. "She'll wish her cake dough afore she's done of him. There's a bluebeardy look about 'en; and 'twill out in time."

"Stuff—he's well enough! Some folk want their luck buttered. If I had a choice as wide as the ocean sea I wouldn't wish for a better man. A poor twanking woman like her—'tis a godsend for her, and hardly a pair of jumps or night-rail to her name."[164]

The methods remain rudimentary, but the highly flavored speech eventually becomes a means rather than an end. There is of course nothing rudimentary about such a command of language as this; the rustics acquire, eventually, some of the concentrated wit of the Shakespearean fools. After *Under the Greenwood Tree* Hardy rarely tried to reproduce dialect with any exactness and rarely indulged in the weary humor of mere garrulity. But even in that early novel the phrase-by-phrase brilliance, and the sense given through phrasing of the mind's actual movement, more than compensated for an unrestraint which was also to a degree Shakespearean. Like Shakespeare, Hardy sometimes found it hard to drop a joke. But the rustics could be incisive even when they seemed most diffuse:

"Thou'st ought to be able to onriddle such a little chiel as she," the tranter observed.

"The littler the maid, the bigger the riddle, to my mind. And coming of such a stock, too, she may well be a twister."

"Yes; Geoffrey Day is a clever man if ever there was one. Never says anything: not he."

"Never."

"You might live wi' that man, my sonnies, a hundred years, and never know there was anything in him."

"Ay; one o' these up-country London ink-bottle fellers would call Geoffrey a fool."

"Ye never find out what's in that man: never," said Spinks.

"Silent? ah, he is silent! He can keep silence well. That man's silence is wonderful to listen to."

"There's so much sense in it. Every moment o' it is brimmen over wi' sound understanding."

" 'A can keep a very clever silence—very clever, truly," echoed Leaf. " 'A do look at me as if 'a could see my thoughts running like the works of a clock."

"Well, all will agree that the man can halt well in his talk, be it a long time or be it a short time. And though we can't expect his daughter to inherit his dumbness, she may have a few dribblets from his sense."

"And his pocket, perhaps."

"Yes; the nine hundred pound that everybody says he's worth; but I call it four hundred and fifty; for I never believe more than half I hear."[165]

"Fate's nothen beside a woman's schemen," Clerk Crickett says in Hardy's first published novel. "Doom is nothing beside an elderly woman—quite a chiel in her hands," Geoffrey Day says in his second. Hardy's ability to create personality out of whole cloth and literary reminiscence is obvious in even the least interesting of the rustics. But his ability to evoke feminine personality, which is distinctly less "literary," is even more striking. Few novelists, English or Continental, have such a gallery of charming, impulsive, and dangerously contradictory women to their credit; Hardy was certainly the greatest dramatist of female character and temperament in a half-century almost monopolized by female novelists. He was the recorder of evasive personalities, the analyst of such psychic difficulties as Sue's, the creator of rounded characters as different as Eustacia Vye and Tess—and a most cynical theorist *de natura feminae*. His attitude progressed, as we have seen, from fascinated and unwillingly sympathetic criticism to almost uncritical sympathy, but his view of woman's incorrigible nature long remained unchanged. He made at the outset a rectilinear judgment on the complex, variable, and admittedly obscure. The wonder is that proceeding from such a definite judgment and position, he could achieve so much amusing variety. This once at least he was not crippled by his preconceptions—perhaps because they were fairly sound ones, though certainly incomplete. The incompleteness may be put in this way: Whereas Hardy *chose* to see the rustics only in terms of personality, leaving more serious treatment to the poems, he was at first *unable* to see feminine character except as personality. He looked upon his women from the outside coolly and as the sum of their illogical evasions. Thus Cytherea Graye, Fancy Day, and Elfride Swancourt (who would alone suffice to make another novelist's reputation) are incomplete beside Tess Durbeyfield and Sue Bridehead.

Woman has, in Santayana's words, a sibylline intuition and the right to be irrationally apropos. Hardy emphasizes rather woman's impulse to seize the day as against man's stubborn idealism. "I am content to build happiness on any accidental basis that may be near at hand," Elfride tells Stephen Smith; "you are for making a world to suit your happiness." "You are just like all women," Clym tells Eustacia; "they are ever content to build their lives on any incidental position that offers itself; whilst men would fain make a globe to suit them." From this first radical difference all others may be said to follow: woman's "impulsive inconsequence," her vanity, her fickleness, her indifference to justice, and her inability to make an unsexed judgment, even her stoical endurance and her curious masochistic impulses. She who lives in an eternal present lives not the life of reason:

In justice to desponding men, it is as well to remember that the brighter endurance of women at these epochs—invaluable, sweet, angelic, as it is—owes more of its origin to a narrower vision that shuts out many of the leaden-eyed despairs in the van, than to a hopefulness intense enough to quell them. . .

Perhaps the moral compensation for all a woman's petty cleverness under thriving conditions is the real nobility that lies in her extreme foolishness at these other times; her sheer inability to be simply just, her exercise of an illogical power entirely denied to men in general—the power not only of kissing, but of delighting to kiss the rod by a punctilious observance of the self-immolating doctrines in the Sermon on the Mount.[166]

Men, idealists, are ever determined to project their dreams and egos into a reasonable future; they are determined to turn the stream of events. But even tenderness in women is "accompanied by a sort of self-committal to the stream of events." Where men see the dream behind reality and patiently await its realization, women take the dream for reality and abandon themselves to the first illusion that presents itself. Are irrational women the only reasonable beings in an irrational universe that recks not of man's longing for order? The staple Hardy plot juxtaposes a dogged idealist and a volatile woman who flutters ambiguously about him; the man waits patiently for the woman to settle down and lead a reasonable life. But it is not in woman's nature to settle down. Not merely Dick Dewy but many another faithful Wessex lover would have escaped much discomfort had he shared the elder Dewy's wisdom: "Now, Dick, this is how a maid is. She'll swear she's dying for thee, and she is dying for thee, and she will die for thee; but she'll fling a look over t'other shoulder at another young feller, though never leaving off dying for thee just the same."[167]

Elfride Swancourt and Anne Garland and how many others live in the present, and therefore prefer energy to generosity and merit. Since they do live in the present, they cannot recognize any merit in self-denial and unaggressiveness, which imply a compensating future. "His very kindness in letting her return was his offence. Elfride had her sex's love of sheer force in a man, however ill-directed." Women, incorrigibly bent on enjoying life, are unmoral, and by the same token charming. They are as unmoral and charming as any other irrational, unregenerate objects. They are scarcely to be "understood" and must therefore be pardoned.

These are the preconceptions implicit in the early novels; a logical rationale, very nearly, of feminine evasion and fickleness. In *Far from the Madding Crowd* and later novels Hardy was both more comprehensive and more charitable, though he seldom wholly relaxed his amused distrust. He saw that women as well as men could be ploddingly faithful to a dream. The oversimplified view of the early novels nevertheless had its very real value. Given the astounding passivity and shy backwardness of Edward Springrove, Dick Dewy, and Stephen Smith, was not a certain amount of unpredictable perversity and aggressiveness demanded from the heroines, if only to advance the plots?

"I didn't mean to stop you quite," she faltered with some alarm; and seeing that he still remained silent, she added more anxiously, "If you say that again, perhaps I will not be quite—quite so obstinate—if—if you don't like me to be."

"Oh, my Elfride!" he exclaimed, and kissed her.[168]

The women of these early novels are willing to live and therefore come to life; the men do not come to life, since they are content to dream and wait. Hardy was not a highly subjective novelist and gave little promise that he would some day write *The Mayor of Casterbridge;* elsewhere, the women save his plots. It could further be argued that the oversimplified view focused Hardy's attention on the minutiae of feminine conduct to an extraordinary degree and energized that attention. Starting from the assumption that women are irrational, impulsive, vain, fickle, dishonest, and unjust, Hardy looked for minute signs and gestures of self-betrayal. He saw, examining personality rather than character, how a young woman's mind worked; he listened to the way young women talked. And he was fascinated as well as shocked by what he heard.

His remarkable ear for feminine tones—coy, artful, or evasive—is manifest even in the stumbling early pages of *Desperate Remedies.* Cytherea Graye's is a skillful portrait of a girl whose world is "tolerably vacant," and who is ready to fall in love even before first sight. The mere mention of Mr. Gradfield's draughtsman calls forth a volley of questions, of which the fourth only is, "What would he wish his wife to be like?" Less than three weeks later she is so in love with the draughtsman that she cannot even steer a rowboat straight, and feels for the first time in her life the "charming sensation of being compelled into an opinion by a man she loved." The interview between Cytherea and Adelaide Hinton, on whom she calls to collect a church subscription, is an astounding display of virtuosity, as good in its way as anything in the later books.[169] Like every proper young lady, Cytherea assumes that Adelaide's casually mentioned "friend" is a woman, but decides to the contrary on the mere evidence that no woman would evoke the phrase "humorous reproof." It requires less than a page for Cytherea to learn that the friend is a lover, that Adelaide is engaged to him, that they are to be married in two months, and that the man is very probably Edward Springrove. In startling contrast with that dreary draughtsman and with the stagy Aeneas Manston, all the women in the book are alive. The experienced are as convincing as the innocent. The personality of Eunice, a down at the heels American actress, is evoked by a few lines from a gloomy letter of complaint:

MY DEAR HUSBAND,—Why don't you write? Do you hate me? I have not had the heart to do anything this last week. That I, your wife, should be in this strait, and my husband well to do! I have been obliged to leave my first lodging for debt—among other things, they charged me for a lot of brandy which I am quite sure I did not taste. Then I went to Camberwell and was found out by them. I went away privately from thence, and changed my name the second time. I am now Mrs. Rondley. But the new lodging was the wretchedest and dearest I ever set foot in and I left it after being there only a day. I am now at No. 20 in the same street that you left me in originally. All last night the sash of my window rattled so dreadfully that I could not sleep, but I had not energy enough to get out of bed to stop it. This morning I have been walking—I don't know how far—but far enough to make my feet ache. I have been looking at the outside of two or three of the theatres, but they seem forbidding if I regard them with the eye of an actress in search of an engagement. Though you said I was to think no more of the stage, I believe you would not care if you found me there . . . The idea of being brought on as far as London and then left here alone! Why didn't you leave me in Liverpool?[170]

"If she'd been rale wexwork she couldn't ha' been comelier." Such is Michael Mail's immediate judgment on Fancy Day, the second of Hardy's pert ingénues and slightly dubious heroines. Fancy is perhaps the only one of these heroines whose fickleness seems a trifle theoretical; her quick acceptance of Mr. Maybold, though engaged to Dick Dewy and in love with him, is simply not credible. Did Hardy want to say that feminine behavior is *not* credible? Or did he see no other way to make his point than to have Fancy make it herself, in a letter of retraction?

It is my nature—perhaps all women's—to love refinement of mind and manners; but even more than this, to be ever fascinated with the idea of surroundings more elegant and luxurious than those which have been customary. And you praised me, and praise is life to me. It was alone my sensations at these things which prompted my reply. Ambition and vanity they would be called; perhaps they are so.[171]

Except at this brief moment, Fancy is always believable. But she is also an extreme example of created living personality as opposed to created living character. She is an appearance, a voice, a quick wit, a series of charming gestures—an unmistakeable presence. "An easy bend of neck and graceful set of head; full and wavy bundles of dark-brown hair; light fall of little feet; pretty devices on the skirt of the dress; clear deep eyes; in short, a bunch of sweets: it was Fancy!" And Fancy is no more than this. She has no inner life, no "character" beyond this minxish personality to determine what she shall or shall not do, no past history or future. Thus slightly endowed, she nevertheless dominates the book. "I think I can manage any vicar's views about me if he's under forty," she remarks with some justice, when told that Mr. Maybold would disapprove of a muslin dress. She manages Dick beautifully at an impromptu tea party, though provided with only one cup and saucer, one spoon, and one basin of water for washing their hands. Their four hands get "mixed up" in the basin, but Fancy is not one for further self-effacement:

"The kettle boils; now you shall have a cup of tea," said Fancy, diving into the hamper she had brought.

"Thank you," said Dick, whose drive had made him ready for a cup, especially in her company.

"Well, here's only one cup and saucer, as I breathe! Whatever could mother be thinking about. Do you mind making shift, Mr. Dewy?"

"Not at all, Miss Day," said that civil person.

"—And only having a cup by itself? or a saucer by itself?"

"Don't mind in the least."

"Which do you mean by that?"

"I mean the cup, if you like the saucer."

"And the saucer, if I like the cup?"

"Exactly, Miss Day."

"Thank you, Mr. Dewy, for I like the cup decidedly."[172]

When at last the tea is ready, Fancy must also get the conversation underway, something the dull-witted and adoring Dick could never be expected to do. She gazes out the window with "large lost eyes" and murmurs, "Nobody seems to care about me"—one remark at least which is splendidly and irrationally apropos.

Dick Dewy cannot understand why Fancy should spend an entire afternoon dressing for a nutting excursion which she then has no time to take; very few of these placid Wessex lovers understand their Fancy Days, who are too "inconsequent" if not too good for them. Hardy's heroines might be described academically as victims of "psychic unemployment," or even as examples of "conspicuous waste." Elfride Swancourt, who at first seems no more than a pair of blue eyes, is in fact a minor Eustacia Vye, full of unused feminine energies; herself a Queen of the Night, restlessly pacing the fog-bound Cornwall coast. Like Eustacia, she dispenses permissions to kiss her hand with an untutored but queenly despotism; confronted by such shambling and backward lovers, even her innocence is dangerous. How could she have known that giving Felix Jethway permission to hold her pony, when others had offered their services first, would eventually cause him to die of love? Compared with Fancy Day, Elfride desires power rather than praise—a first significant step, perhaps, in Hardy's changing view of women; in the transition from personality to character. But her darting feminine reasonings and tones are as convincing as Fancy's. She is annoyed because Stephen Smith talks so much about Henry Knight:

"I don't care how good he is; I don't want to know him, because he comes between me and you. You think of him night and day, ever so much more than of anybody else; and when you are thinking of him, I am shut out of your mind."

"No, dear Elfride; I love you dearly."

"And I don't like you to tell me so warmly about him when you are in the middle of loving me. Stephen, suppose that I and this man Knight of yours were both drowning, and you could only save one of us—"

"Yes—the stupid old proposition—which would I save?"

"Well, which? Not me."

"Both of you," he said, pressing her pendent hand.

"No, that won't do; only one of us."

"I cannot say; I don't know. It is disagreeable—quite a horried idea to have to handle."

"A-ha, I know. You would save him, and let me drown, drown, drown; and I don't care about your love."[173]

Elfride finally forces Stephen to admit that he would let Knight drown. Not many months later, seated with Knight on the spot where she had lost an earring while kissing Stephen, she forces her new lover to admit that he prefers blue eyes to hazel ones. She has just accepted a new pair of earrings from Knight and permits him to kiss her:

"Ah, we must be careful! I lost the other earring doing like this."

No sooner did she realise the significant words than a troubled look passed across her face, and she shut her lips as if to keep them back.

"Doing like what?" said Knight, perplexed.

"Oh, sitting down out of doors," she replied hastily.[174]

Hardy's first and second novels showed surprising knowledge of girlish coquetries and mannerisms; much later novels would show insight as surprising into feminine motives and feelings. *A Pair of Blue Eyes* offers, however, a curious midpoint of knowledge, which one can only call a knowledge of the feminine nervous temperament. Toward the end of the novel Hardy himself discriminates between Elfride's nature (gentle, confiding, and innocent) and her personality (vain, evasive, and ambiguous). Hardy was often tempted to generalize about all women from the particular woman at hand, as Conrad to generalize about all men. "Woman's ruling passion—to fascinate those more powerful than she—though operant in Elfride, was decidedly purposeless." As we reëxamine each crisis from the vantage point of Hardy's final sympathy, the "purposeless" character of Elfride's betrayals becomes evident enough. It is a trick of excited nerves that throws her into Knight's arms a moment after she has saved his life; later she shows a nervous rather than moral inability to confess her sins. Much earlier the mere "act of alighting upon strange ground" in London was sufficient to induce a *crise de nerfs* and send her back to Endelstow unmarried. Paddington has disillusioned many a traveler both before Elfride and since. But few novelists have caught so well, in dialogue, the sheer revolt of nerves which so many women feel at the threshold of a new life. In three compact pages we have a first sketch of a situation which would be complicated and subtilized in *Jude the Obscure* and charged not with pathos but horror.[175]

Was this already, rather than Knight's cross-examination, the turning point of Hardy's sympathy? The characterization of Elfride is an incomplete one, since the true origin of the sympathy seems to exist somewhere outside the book itself. The reader, in any event, can hardly share that sympathy. But sympathy—something more, that is, than the cool observation of women as fascinating objects—would be necessary to the later and universally praised portraits of Eustacia Vye and Tess Durbeyfield. Hardy's sympathy, however unmotivated in *A Pair of Blue Eyes,* is justified in *Far from the Madding Crowd.* Bathsheba Everdene, at first another Fancy Day, a vain and highly amusing tease, becomes almost a symbolic figure of resourcefulness and endurance. Less obviously striking than Cytherea, Fancy, and Elfride, and perhaps even less alive than they, she is the first of Hardy's heroines to face her life at all squarely. She is the first of his women to show more character than personality. In the most interesting women, in Sue Bridehead for instance, personality and character coincide. Sue's bird-like mannerisms and mobile features are a true index to her nervous disorders, which in turn *are* her character to a very considerable degree.

The conflict between the impulse to create personality and the impulse to create character appears for the last time in the portrait of Eustacia Vye, who is also the first of Hardy's irresponsible and mildly neurotic hedonists. A great deal that is obviously successful in the portrait no longer need be discussed: the sense that it gives of a presence brooding dangerously over the fortunes of more docile persons in the valley below—a presence equipped with bonfire and telescope; the impression of unused baffled energies and a recklessly masculine intellect; the conveyed despair and loneliness that will make any bargain to escape the heath; the desperate clawing for love as the only form of pleasure known; the pride, which refuses to explain away misleading appearances; the harsh honesty, finally, of a direct appraisal of self. The famous seventh chapter, "Queen of Night," will still repay the attention of any student of Hardy's development, however, for it is not merely an attempt to create character through personality but also an attempt to create personality through grandiose impressionism. Could the large methods which had been used to evoke the totality of Egdon Heath be applied to a mere nineteen-year-old girl—still a girl, though she might someday sit between the Héloïses and the Cleopatras? The impressionism, which leaps daringly from pedantic meditations on the gods to minute descriptions of hair fillets and hair, reminds one of Pater's prose poem on the Gioconda, published five years before. Hardy's prose poem created its desired and dark effect, however obvious its methods may seem on a third or fourth reading. The wonder is rather that the subsequent and more orthodox portrait should have been able to survive such an overwhelming first impression. The eight seemingly diffuse but in fact very close pages dwell on Eustacia's appearance, moral isolation, and larger "nocturnal mysteries." But they also manage to take in, almost parenthetically, the important facts of her childhood and heredity, of her daily way of life, of her idealizing love for Wildeve. The statement is so full as to threaten any further appearance of Eustacia with commonplaceness and redundancy. But the portrait does survive—and not least in its curious ability to suggest savage and even immoral feeling without recourse to much unconventional behavior. It required unusual tact, for instance, to make Eustacia's giving of her hand to Charley to kiss, for a certain number of minutes, the sleaziest of bargains. The general impression of darkness achieved apart from particular dark deeds is so strong that Hardy feels obliged to summarize it explicitly only once: "As far as social ethics were concerned Eustacia approached the savage state, though in emotion she was all the while an epicure. She had advanced to the secret recesses of sensuousness, yet had hardly crossed the threshold of conventionality."[176]

Hardy's characterizations of young women are rarely ambiguous and with the single exception of Sue Bridehead require no interpretation. There is little to say about them individually that has not already been said abundantly and often. These women do, on the other hand, fall into fairly distinct groups—the sweet ingénues, the restless hedonists, the patient and enduring sufferers, and so forth—and the relationships among and within these groups are worth some attention. To chart these groupings is to observe at once how steadily Hardy progressed toward a dramatization of character rather than personality; and toward frankness as well as charity (see chart, page 141). All novelists tend to borrow from their earlier works, though as a rule unconsciously. Hardy's tendency to do this was particularly strong. One could almost say, given the degree to which women dominate his stories, that nearly every novel had its source in some trait, perhaps unemphasized or undeveloped, of the preceding novel's heroine. Thus Cytherea Graye's inability to choose the right man becomes in Fancy Day a rather astounding fickleness. Fancy, far more vain than Cytherea, passes on both her fickleness and her still fairly innocent pride to Elfride Swancourt, in whom evasiveness becomes systematic, sombre, and at last of tragic consequence. Elfride in turn is not merely vain, proud, and vacillating, but is also intelligent and in a sense irrespressible; she almost survives the holocaust. Bathsheba Everdene of the early chapters inherits all Elfride's qualities, and her teasing dismissal of Oak's first proposal marks the farthest point Hardy would go in this single and amusing but rather conventional direction of satire. There was no more to be said about mere girlish vanity, but there was much else about women that had not been said. What would the intelligence and even strength of Elfride have amounted to had they overcome her youthful inconsequence? What would *she* have amounted to, had she been thrown on her own resources and forced to make a living? These questions take us at once into the later chapters of *Far from the Madding Crowd.* The matured Bathsheba may have to depend on Oak at critical hours, but she is a courageous figure in her own right. She has been changed by responsibility and disaster. She passes on much of her courage, resourcefulness, and determination to survive to the grasping and harsh Ethelberta; but passes on very little of her honesty and none of her early charm. Did Ethelberta's unmoral pursuit of power and wealth suggest, finally, Eustacia's unmoral pursuit of pleasure?

There are other links between the various books as curious as these, and to list Hardy's women is to construct a more than figurative genealogy. Felice Charmond not merely follows Lucetta Le Sueur, but is descended directly from her, inheriting her bored restlessness, her aura of foreign and unmoral glamor, her slightly faded vivacity, and even her French-sounding name. She does

THE GENEALOGY OF HARDY'S YOUNGER WOMEN

An illustration of the way in which many of Hardy's women characters draw on their predecessors and even derive directly from them

NOVELS	THE VAIN AND FICKLE	THE INGÉNUES	THE AVERAGE INTELLIGENT WOMEN	THE HEDONISTS TENDING TO NEUROSIS	THE HIGHLY SEXED	THE RESOURCEFUL AND ENDURING	TWO PURE WOMEN
Desperate Remedies, '71	Cytherea		Cytherea				
Greenwood Tree, '72	Fancy Day						
Blue Eyes, '73	Elfride						
Madding Crowd, '74	The early Bathsheba					The later Bathsheba	
Ethelberta, '76	The early Ethelberta	Picotee				The later Ethelberta	
Return, '78		Thomasin		Eustacia	Eustacia		
Trumpet-Major, '80		Anne					
Laodicean, '81			Paula				
Two on a Tower, '82		Tabitha	Viviette				
Milkmaid, '83		Margery					
Mayor, '86			Elizabeth	Lucetta			
Woodlanders, '87			Grace	Felice	Suke	Marty	Marty
Tess, '91					Tess	Tess	Tess
Well-Beloved, '92	Avice II	Avice I	Avice III	Marcia			
Jude, '95				Sue	Arabella	Arabella	

not inherit, however, Lucetta's status as a victim, and so receives much less sympathy than she. Did Hardy ask himself what kind of mischief such a person as Lucetta might cause if thrust into an even more cloistered environment than Casterbridge? A novelist rarely asks himself such direct questions, but he does work under direct though subconscious obligations: to pursue the ideas he has only half explored, the feelings only half expressed, the characters only half realized and *tested.*

A novel may be in direct reaction against the preceding one, but it nearly always proceeds out of it in some discernible way—especially since a true novelist can hardly exhaust his intentions in a single book. The connections between *The Woodlanders* and *Tess of the D'Urbervilles,* for instance, may at first glance seem fairly tenuous, fining down to nothing more specific than the contrast between urban corruptness and rural innocence and the close common dependence of the characters on physical nature for their living. Yet Tess herself is directly descended from Marty South, and even perhaps from Suke Damson. Suke merely stands on the squalid fringes of the story, a highly sexed and unreflective hoyden who casually gives herself to the rakish Dr. Fitzpiers. Marty, on the other hand, is a "pure woman" as well as a hard-working and unselfish child of the soil; she is betrayed only in the sense that Giles never appreciates her solid worth and fidelity. But what would have happened had Marty been endowed with Suke's sensuous nature as well as her own purity and faithfulness? What would have happened had *she* been seduced by an intruding Dr. Fitzpiers? And what, finally, must have been the inner life of such a simple and pure child of the soil, seduced or unseduced? To answer these questions about Marty South, consciously or unconsciously, is to conceive of Tess Durbeyfield.

All groupings are to a degree arbitrary, however, and must be looked on with unremittent distrust. Both Tess and Arabella, for instance, are simple, uneducated, and sensuously ample women, and both show astounding endurance. But it would be manifestly absurd to argue that one character suggested the other. The significance of their close juxtaposition (the two lease epicene of Hardy's women) consists rather in the changing public attitude toward the treatment of sexual impulses in fiction. It could be argued at last that ethics went beyond the single problem of chastity; that the devirginated could be pure or impure. The only other possible connection between the two characters may lie in a possible desire to correct an exaggerated impression. Hardy (who had once argued the innocence of all rustics, servant girls, etc.) may have wanted to acknowledge, however belatedly, that it takes all kinds to make even a Wessex world. He could not in all conscience let Tess and her dairymaid friends stand as his final portraits of female rural character.

The groupings nevertheless remain valid and useful even after a detailed surview of Hardy's women has been taken; certain traits and types unmistakably recur. The obvious progress was from an assumption that all young women are unpredictable in the same amusing way to an understanding that women may differ one from the other as much as men do and may even be as purposeful and idealistic as they. To the last Hardy's women never lose their feminine mannerisms and may revert to startling inconsequence; even Marty South and Tess can never become as stolid as Gabriel Oak or as colorlessly passive as Stephen Smith. But the heroine who is above all vain and fickle disappears almost completely from the novels—though she makes a few last and perverse appearances in *A Group of Noble Dames.* The group of sweet, passive ingénues is the most distinct and the least interesting of all. Like all women they are incapable of making unsexed judgments and so usually choose the wrong men. They are rather unintelligent but neither selfish nor perverse; they might all have been the parson's younger daughter who did not write a novel. They are victims when exposed to the rakes, but make the unaggressive Diggory Venns and John Lovedays their unintentional victims. What of any significance distinguishes Picotee from Thomasin or Thomasin from Anne Garland? Tabitha Lark, a mere pert and blooming presence bounding healthfully across a field, might well be considered the reduction to nonenity of the conventional ingénue.

To describe Paula Power, Viviette Constantine, Elizabeth-Jane Newson, and Grace Melbury as average intelligent women is to beg the one interesting question of their everyday realism. Yet it would be still more misleading to call them average women or intelligent women. They belong to the class of the unclassified not because they are highly individualized, which they are not, but because they have no very prominent traits. They are neither selfish nor exceptionally generous, neither stupid nor remarkably intelligent, neither highly sexed nor epicene. They are ordinary English women, examined with quiet ordinary realism, and their interest thus depends almost exclusively on the mishaps that befall them. With luck as commonplace as her own character was commonplace, Baptista Trewthen of "A Mere Interlude" might have drifted through the most uneventful of cloistered lives. As it is, her indifferent drifting character provokes one of Hardy's finest comedies: a long short story which deserves a much wider audience than it has ever won. On the way to marry one man she drifts into marriage with another, and accepts the fact of his drowning a few hours later with a rather astounding calm. She does the calm sensible thing, which is to go ahead with her original plan. It is mere mischance that brings her, on her second wedding night, to the room from which the body of her first husband had just been removed and where his hat was still to be found. In the end she does confess, sensibly enough. Her husband in turn makes his own confession: he has by an earlier wife four termagant daughters, whom Baptista will be obliged to raise.

As a rule the women of the short stories and novelettes resist obvious classification more often than do those of the novels. It is hard to see why this should be so, unless a brief glance fixes on obvious individuality, while full exploration goes beyond it to the type: to what has already been observed and often. The homesick Sophy of "The Son's Veto," the frustrated Mrs. Harnham of "On the Western Circuit," the independent Mrs. Frankland of "For Conscience' Sake," the hysterical Car'line of "The Fiddler of the Reels"—these and many others refuse to fit any of the broad categories. Lizzy Newberry of "The Distracted Preacher" (1879, *Wessex Tales)* makes that novelette one of Hardy's most successful comedies. She is certainly more independent than any of her contemporaries in the novels, with the exception of Eustacia Vye; she is a very unmoral young lady who smuggles rum for fun rather than profit and who takes in the new Methodist preacher as a boarder. Do we not have here, once again, Hardy's inevitable contrast between the lively engaging heroine and the dull moralizing hero? When her preacher catches cold, Lizzy has only to broach one of the tubs of rum hidden in the cellar of the church and refill it with water. The real Lizzy, according to a note of 1912, did not reform and did not marry the minister. Hardy regretted that the conventional ending had been "almost *de rigueur* in an English magazine at the time of writing." Lizzy has this only in common with Hardy's other heroines: she is more interesting than the man who loves her.

The women, whatever their perverse absurdities, are also more plausible than the men. Hardy's was a world of young women and girls, but even the older women hovering in the background of his achievement are convincing and individualized: the severe and haunted Miss Aldclyffe; the superstitious Rhoda Brook; the faded and naïve Susan Henchard; Mrs. Yeobright, grasping her son's affection. Hardy's women, young or old, unfailingly betray themselves by some radically feminine impulse which another novelist would have ignored; by some characteristic gesture or some unguarded word. They blunder ahead, creating the circumstances that trap them—while the men go through their dull and predetermined paces. Hardy missed his chance more than once with potentially great characters; most notably with Ethelberta. But the foreground of the achievement is impressive enough. None of Hardy's women are unalive, and very few of them are wholly uninteresting; even the innocent ingénues are capable of occasional violent flareups. Can we approve, finally, such a marked tendency to assign women to types; to present a few similar heroines again and again? For one thing, there are always important differences. The woman deemed to be of a certain temperament is also seen as an individual; Elfride is by no means Fancy Day. More importantly, Hardy's six greatest women characters differ radically among themselves: Elfride, nervous and evasive; Bathsheba, curiously masculine and feminine; the wild, proud, and unreconciled Eustacia; the tender and "pure" Tess; the tormented yet fun-loving Sue; and Arabella, the female animal. Against these six major characters and a host of convincing minor ones, Hardy offers only two men of more than average interest and vitality: Michael Henchard and Jude Fawley.

Henchard, who is Hardy's Lord Jim, stands at the very summit of his creator's achievement; his only tragic hero and one of the greatest tragic heroes in all fiction. He takes his place at once with certain towering and possessed figures of Melville, Hawthorne, and Dostoevsky: a man of character obsessed by guilt and so committed to his own destruction. He anticipates not merely Lord Jim and the Razumov of *Under Western Eyes* but also the Michel of André Gide's *L'Immoraliste.* Fifty years before Karl Menninger, Hardy recognized—as Shakespeare did three centuries before him—that the guilty not merely flagellate themselves but also thrust themselves in the way of bad luck; *create* what appear to be unlucky accidents. Henchard's decline in Casterbridge was no more fortuitous than Lord Jim's in Patusan. These two "men of character" pursued strikingly similar destines: forceful, conscientious, and proud, alike outcasts thanks to the unaccountable flarings of a moment's fear and anger, dedicating their lives to an impossible rehabilitation and a distant ideal of honor. They are isolated and obsessed by guilt even in their fat years of power and prestige; they are determined to bear yet face down the past. Both are men of character in a strangely double sense. They want to atone for the past through self-punishment; yet they resist, humanly, merely compulsive self-punishment. In the end both are paralyzed by "chance" reminders from the past (Brown and the furmity-woman)—reminders which, in fact, they had never ceased to carry about with them. They achieve death in solitude, each having one dull-witted uncomprehending native who remains faithful to the last. Of the two Henchard, whose will was a final self-condemnation, may have shown more courage than Lord Jim, who turned to his executioners and to the world with a last look of proud defiance. Henchard was a "man of character"; Lord Jim was "one of us."

There was nothing in Hardy's earlier novels to suggest that he would some day produce such a figure; there is no series of links and experiments leading from Springrove or Manston to Henchard. Gabriel Oak, Diggory Venn, and many others seem to act perversely against their own interest, but this is owing to meditative impotence and a lack of normal aggressiveness. They are spectators rather than actors against themselves. Unlike them Henchard is a man of great force and destructive energy, which he turns outward occasionally but inward far more often. He has thus nothing in common with the irresponsible Wildeve, but a great deal in common with both Jude and

Sue. There is little justification for the critic who sums up Henchard's tragic flaws as temper and addiction to drink; these were symptoms of the self-destructive impulse rather than its causes. Hardy himself was explicit enough:

Thereupon promptly came to the surface that idiosyncrasy of Henchard's which had ruled his courses from the beginning, and had mainly made him what he was. Instead of thinking that a union between his cherished stepdaughter and the energetic thriving Donald was a thing to be desired for her good and his own, he hated the very possibility.

Among the many hindrances to such a pleading, not the least was this, that he did not sufficiently value himself to lessen his sufferings by strenuous appeal or elaborate argument.

He had not expressed to her any regrets or excuses for what he had done in the past; but it was a part of his nature to extenuate nothing and live on as one of his own worst accusers.[177]

Henchard is simply incapable of acting consistently in his own interest. Captain Ahab, traveling the wide seas in pursuit of his own destruction, supposes cosmic hostilities in a whale. And so Henchard, earthbound in Casterbridge, comes at last to think "some sinister intelligence bent on punishing him." Had someone roasted a wax image of him? Was some power working against him? Unaware that the power was wholly inward, he "looked out at the night as at a fiend."[178]

Thus Hardy, who had seldom troubled himself with crime and punishment, at last explored the great nineteenth-century myth of the isolated, damned, and self-destructive individualist—the more impressively because his Lara, Vautrin, Tito Melema, and Ahab was an ordinary Wessex farmer-merchant. The particular myth was conceived in terms as grand as the Wessex environment would allow—beginning with no less than the angry, drunken, and impulsive sale of a wife on the fairgrounds of Weydon

Priors, to which Henchard would return a quarter of a century later in full circle. The tendency to paranoia and self-flagellation must have had its origin, like that of Sue Bridehead, in some part of an undisclosed childhood. At the very beginning Henchard has already the "instinct of a perverse character"; he drinks too much and thinks he has ruined his chances by marrying at eighteen. It is the crime of selling his wife which concentrates his energies, however; which both makes his character and destroys it. (Here too he is exactly like Lord Jim, who might have remained, in innocence, a fairly ordinary sea captain and trader.) Henchard looks in vain for his wife; swears an oath not to drink for twenty years; becomes mayor of Casterbridge, though equipped with little more than energy—becomes a man of character. When Susan finally reappears, he stolidly and conscientiously marries her; when Lucetta reappears, he acts honorably, though long tempted to revenge himself on Farfrae through her; when the furmity-woman reappears, he publicly acknowledges his guilt. He is fair in his savage fashion, and fights Farfrae with one hand tied behind his back. Ruined, he is the most conscientious of bankrupts.

The Mayor of Casterbridge is a novel of temperament in action, in minute action even; its distinction derives from a severe concentration on the self-destructive aspects of that temperament. The obligation to punish and degrade the self is at times fairly conscious. Thus Henchard marries Susan not merely to make amends to her and to provide Elizabeth-Jane with a home, but also "to castigate himself with the thorns which these restitutory acts brought in their train; among them the lowering of his dignity in public opinion by marrying so comparatively humble a woman." He licks his wounds by demanding that the journeymen sing the terrible One Hundred and Ninth Psalm; he goes to work for Farfrae wearing the rusty silk hat of his former dignity; he humbles himself unnecessarily before Lucetta; he lingers on the second stone bridge where the failures and drifters of the town gather.[179] But Hardy recognized, intuitively at least, that the guilty may also punish themselves unconsciously and cause their own "bad luck." The man who repeatedly cuts and burns himself is no mere victim of absurd mischance; he is compelled to cut and burn himself, though he may not understand his compulsion. Freud has documented the hidden psychology of errors; Menninger the motives of chronic failures and of those who suffer repeated "accidents." Psychologists have proved that the unfortunate are more often than not the guilty, who must pay daily hostages to their fear.

Henchard is such a man, for whom everything "goes wrong" once he has begun to struggle with his guilt. So his elaborate public entertainment fails dismally while Farfrae's modest one succeeds. Rain does not fall at the beck of the accusing conscience, but Henchard's party is ruined by more than rain. "A man must be a headstrong stunpoll to think folk would go up to that bleak place today." Later he gambles on disastrous rains to drive up the price of corn and is confirmed in his prophecy by the mysterious Mr. Fall; he buys enormous quantities of corn and is ruined by the blazing August weather. But the adverse force was his own lack of Wessex prudence. "He was reminded of what he had well known before, that a man might gamble upon the square green areas of fields as readily as upon those of a card-room . . . 'For you can never be sure of weather till 'tis past.' " Henchard's subconscious self-destructiveness shows itself far less equivocally at the time of the Royal Progress. He has a "passing fancy" to join in welcoming the royal visitor, though no longer a member of the town council. But what might have appeared a last conscious effort to reassert his dignity was in fact a half-conscious effort to degrade himself before the collected townfolk in the most humiliating way. "He was not only a journeyman, unable to appear as he formerly had appeared, but he disdained to appear as well as he might. Everybody else, from the Mayor to the washerwoman, shone in new vesture according to means; but Henchard had doggedly retained the fretted and weather-beaten garments of bygone years." And he was drunk. When he resumed drinking after twenty years, a short time before this, he had committed himself to focal suicide and certain self-punishment. Character is fate; and Newson and the furmity-woman, those symbolic reminders, were part of his character and fate. Henchard would have destroyed himself even had they not returned. As a man of character he was morally obligated to do so. Yet he was also obligated to resist mere compulsive self-destructiveness. Here too, in fighting his suicidal destiny, he was a man of character.

Thus grandly and minutely conceived, Henchard might yet have remained as wooden as Farmer Boldwood. But he is very nearly the most personalized of Hardy's men: a voice and an unforgettable massive presence, with his twitching mouth and distant gaze, his "vehement" gloominess, his severe friendliness, and his businesslike bluntness even when proposing marriage. No doubt it is as a well-meaning man isolated by guilt that he makes his strongest appeal to our sympathy. Loneliness as well as guilt prompts him to hire Farfrae impulsively and to pour out his confession at once. And guilt as well as loneliness attaches him to Elizabeth-Jane: "He had liked the look of her face as she answered him from the stairs. There had been affection in it, and above all things what he desired now was affection from anything that was good and pure."[180] Finally, though his history is highly selective, we have the impression that we know Henchard's life in its every significant detail. The measure of the characterization's success is our unquestioning acceptance in its context of Henchard's stylized and symbolic will. It does not seem to us a gratuitous or merely ornamental offering of Hardy's pessimism, as a few of Jude Fawley's philosophical speeches do. Michael Henchard's excommunication of self is a reasoned one, for his life has actually so added up:

> That Elizabeth-Jane Farfrae be not told of
> my death, or made to grieve on account of me.
> & that I be not bury'd in consecrated ground.
> & that no sexton be asked to toll the bell.
> & that nobody is wished to see my dead body.
> & that no murners walk behind me at my funeral.
> & that no flours be planted on my grave.
> & that no man remember me.
> To this I put my name.[181]

"Let the day perish wherein I was born, and the night in which it was said, There is a manchild conceived"—Jude Fawley might have signed Henchard's will.

Jude is not, however, a tragic hero—if only because he is a "modern." Henchard's will is a final condemnation of self and of the "old mankind"; it is an achievement of the self-knowledge which tragedy compels. Jude's dying words are instead a condemnation of the cosmos in its dark and at last recognized absurdity. Not Jude but the cosmos is to blame. There are certain obvious links between the two characters: the common sensitiveness to music, the imprudent early marriages, the addiction to drink, the need to punish and degrade the self publicly. But the significant link occurs in the final paragraph of *The Mayor of Casterbridge;* in Elizabeth-Jane's observation "that neither she nor any human being deserved less than was given." The observation is pathetic and of course pessimistic in the commoner sense of that word. But it is not tragic, as all but the last pages of the novel are tragic. For the tragic attitude lays the blame not on the stars but on ourselves; it sees fate in character; its pessimism is grounded in the insufficiency of the human endowment; it insists, with Conrad's Marlow, that "nobody is good enough."[182] Jude is a victim of his society and inheritance and of a bad luck for which he is only in part responsible. He appeals to our sympathy more than Henchard does, but not merely because of his greater idealism and tenderness. For he appeals to our human indolence, our refusal to take the blame.

These are philosophical reasonings and therefore hardly likely to trouble the casual reader. There are further and more direct reasons why Jude should seem less tragic than Henchard. He does not resist the outward and inward destiny of his actual life as stubbornly as Henchard does; he drifts into disaster. He lacks Henchard's "certain magnitude," which is the magnitude both of a bull and of a rock. More importantly, he cannot resist or overcome his function in the book, which is arbitrary as well as symbolic. A self-educated Mellstock orphan, he must carry the rather distinct overburden of John Stuart Mill's personal struggle with Victorian prudery (which was certainly in Hardy's mind) as well as his own burden of insufficient opportunity. He must serve as a passive victim and foil to the animal Arabella and the epicene Sue, to the irrational institution of marriage, to the academic snobbishness of Christminster, to the late nineteenth century in particular and to "heredity" and the unjust cosmos in general. The cosmos, whether just or unjust or indifferent, necessarily dwarfs tragedy. Finally, Jude must pause—and at the very hours of his most poignant and particular sufferings—to enunciate messages:

"However, it was my poverty and not my will that consented to be beaten. It takes two or three generations to do what I tried to do in one; and my impulses—affections—vices perhaps they should be called—were too strong not to hamper a man without advantages, who should be as cold-blooded as a fish and as selfish as a pig to have a really good chance of being one of his country's worthies . . . I was, perhaps, after all, a paltry victim to the spirit of mental and social restlessness that makes so many unhappy in these days. . . And what I appear, a sick and poor man, is not the worst of me. I am in a chaos of principles—groping in the dark—acting by instinct and not after example. . . I doubt if I have anything more for my present rule of life than following inclinations which do me and nobody else any harm, and actually give pleasure to those I love best."[183]

Jude, for whom self-knowledge came slowly and hard, had

the further obligation to express Hardy's many and random convictions.

He is nevertheless a very substantial character, and the honesty of the record perhaps compensates for the invasion of tragedy by pathos. In this his last novel Hardy finally examines the childhood of one of his heroes; Jude is eleven at the beginning of the book, an orphan cared for by a severe aunt and made to feel he is not wanted. To the modern reader the portrait must seem incomplete in its implication that Jude had no sexual experience or even erotic reveries before the age of nineteen—a curious lacuna to be explained in part by the lateness of Hardy's own development, but also perhaps by the fashions in fiction of the time. The emphasis is rather on the child's sensitiveness, which cannot endure the sight of pain. Curiously enough this was also the point made by Conrad in examining Stevie of *The Secret Agent,* the only child of any importance in his novels—though Conrad went much further than Hardy in explaining the origin of the sensitiveness. The child Jude—who even tiptoes to avoid crushing earthworms—cannot bear to frighten the birds away from Farmer Troutham's field, as he has been employed to do: "They seemed, like himself, to be living in a world which did not want them." This childhood experience is echoed in the famous chapter of the pig-sticking and finally in the story of the rabbit caught in a gin; it is intended to explain Jude's excessive considerateness toward Arabella. "Never such a tender fool as Jude is if a woman seems in trouble, and coaxes him a bit. Just as he used to be about birds and things." The sentimentality which to Conrad always seemed a moral failing—and at the origin of much skepticism, unfaithfulness, and cruelty—is looked upon by Hardy with a very different eye. He recognized that Jude's sensitiveness made him the certain prey of the ruthless. But he also insisted that there was something wrong with a world which could not use these "finer feelings." He did not question the validity of the feelings themselves, which were so largely his own feelings toward half-frozen fieldfares and the like. He no doubt believed, as many people do, that the child who is kind to birds will be a man just toward men.

The psychological portrait suffers from the book's general overburdening; there is no space for an exhaustive view of anything where everything must be looked at in passing. It suffers also from Hardy's determination to force at every point a contrast between the ideal and the sordid; Jude's psyche (though not Sue's) is as neatly split into the animal and the spiritual as that of any character in one of Dickens' moral tales. Thus Jude's aggressive sexuality is presented as an absurd animal annoyance and anomalous counterweight to his tender idealism, though the two must of course have had a close relationship and presumably a common origin. Like Henchard, Jude is driven to drink by despair and guilt, but by despair and "instinct" even more than by guilt. Though he saw no relationship between Jude's sexuality and his abnormal tenderness, Hardy did recognize that frustrated impulses may find various compensations and devious ones. "I have cured myself of drunkenness, I think, but I never know in what new form a suppressed vice will break out in me!" In the end the drunkenness becomes, as with Henchard, a willed self-destructiveness; only through humiliation is momentary peace to be won. But even the last chapters, though perhaps more moving than anything else in Hardy's work, lack *The Mayor of Casterbridge's* concentration. Hardy was on stronger ground, here at least, in dramatizing Jude's love for Sue, his sense of "the isolation of his own personality," and his incorrigible longing for the life of reason. While the psychological portrait is incomplete and at times unconvincing, the dramatic portrait is uniformly successful. It wins a sympathy which even the portrait of Henchard does not.

For it is thus we remember Jude: as a person doing and saying certain things, rather than as a character defined and understood. We remember him as the child of eleven who looks at the far-off lights of Christminster; and as the youth of twenty-two who wanders at night among the ghostly university buildings; and as the prematurely middle-aged man who, nearing death, returns to Christminster on Rememberance Day—hoping to catch through the open windows a few words of the Latin speeches. We remember too, for all the novel's severe and wholly legitimate concentration on Jude's darker hours, certain curious and personalizing moments of happiness: the outing to Wardour Castle; the tea party at Shaston; Jude bending eagerly over the model of the Valley of Jehosaphat; the trip to the Great Wessex Agricultural Show, where Jude and Sue admire their own model of Cardinal College. It is through such modest pleasures as these, and through his always convincing and often boyish dialogue, that Jude becomes perhaps the most human of Hardy's men and certainly the most likeable.

The "character" survives the book's methodical naturalism and multiplied protests; the "personality" survives the analyzed character. This is not the highest art, of course. For the highest art combines these things; balances (as in the portraits of Henchard and Sue) character and personality, understanding and sympathy. The portrait of Jude nevertheless remains impressive as a fully evoked *life*. And it is a portrait preëminently suited to illustrate Hardy's last meaning, as a novelist, which in retrospect appears to have been his central one: that no human being, in his doomed pursuit of happiness, deserves less than is given; that things not men are to blame; that *everybody* is good enough. This sympathetic message and final consoling optimism, diffused as it is through a dozen novels and through the lives of unpretentious, kindly, and rebuffed people, no doubt provides one clue to Hardy's lasting popularity. For the most popular novelists are also the most charitable ones, except in the very long run; they are those who see man more sinned against than sinning. The message is, as I am compelled to see it, a false one. One must take his stand with the darker moral pessimism of Conrad. But it is difficult to do so; the message, though false, is very nearly irresistible.

For this is the conclusion to which we are driven—that Hardy was a great popular novelist and not a great deliberate artist. The rare popular novelist who also deserves our esteem is perhaps the most difficult one to account for and to analyze. We add up his distinguishable virtues patiently, only to arrive at an absurdly small sum. Dissatisfied with this sum, we posit still other virtues. This is what most of Hardy's critics have done. Starting from a wholly justified liking for the novels, they have gone on to discern the qualities which they assume a great novelist must show: profound thought, high unremittent seriousness of purpose, insight into social problems, exceptional psychological understanding, perfection of structure and style, realism and poetry. But we must look elsewhere than to Hardy for such qualities as these; we must look, for instance, to Conrad at his best. Hardy revealed repeatedly an initial sluggishness of mind, most often perhaps in his tendency to schematize and oversimplify dilemmas. His frank purpose through most of his career was to write books which would sell easily. Although he showed an aesthetic understanding of agricultural Dorset, he showed, prior to *Jude the Obscure,* little understanding of the moral and social condition of the late nineteenth century. His power to dramatize the personality and temperament of women was indeed extraordinary, but he presents fewer interesting men than almost any important novelist. And with the two exceptions of *The Mayor of Casterbridge* and *Under the Greenwood Tree,* his novels are radically imperfect in structure. His style conveys temperament but is abnormally relaxed and diffuse. And for realism and poetry his poems, not his novels, invite us.

His final and unmistakable appeal therefore rests on

much less austere grounds than these: on the popular storytelling of a singularly uninhibited imagination, on an occasional mastery of atmosphere in relation to character, on a variety of manner and mood frankly modeled on Shakespeare's, on a fine purity of temperament—and, above all, on an incorrigible sympathy for all who are lonely and all who long for happiness. He understood the plight of ordinary, simple, and well-meaning persons, subjected to the extraordinary, complex, and seemingly malign circumstances of life. He could find a saving grace in all failure, while Conrad found evil in all success and behind every act of benevolence. Even the heroes of Conrad are subjected to pitiless analysis; the unworthy are looked upon with cold disdain. But which of Hardy's villains is irrevocably damned? And which—Sergeant Troy, Wildeve, Alec D'Urberville, even William Dare—does not benefit at least briefly from this universal sympathy? Hardy's dark vision of the world compelled him, in compensatory fairness, to a certainly excessive charity. Good and evil seemed irrelevant in such an indifferent universe; he wanted people to be happy. He was not concerned with damnation and salvation—as Dostoevsky and Melville and the very greatest writers have been, as Conrad and Gide were to be.

The literary historian and the modern novelist alike can benefit from a study of Hardy's anti-realism and occasional symbolist experiments; they can discover in Hardy ways of escaping inanimate drabness. But it would be absurd to read into Hardy's anti-realism any profound metaphysical intentions, or into his symbolist experiments the complex aesthetic intentions of Conrad. For Hardy did not take his craft seriously in the way that James, Conrad, Proust, and Gide were to take it seriously; he did not conceive of fiction as a high art, at least not until very late; he rested on his poems all claims to uncompromising greatness. Was he finally persuaded by his admirers that novels too could be great works of art? In the end he did write, and seemingly with full consciousness of what he was doing, three very great novels: *Tess of the D'Urbervilles, The Mayor of Casterbridge,* and *Jude the Obscure.* But only two of these explore at all the great theme of nineteenth- and twentieth-century fiction: the myth of the morally isolated individualist lost in a world he never made; who searches for freedom, though bereft of faith, and who wills his own destruction. It would require Conrad, once thought a popular storyteller and historian of simple hearts, to explore the destructive element exhaustively. There will never be too many such exploring pessimists; there will never be too many Conrads. But in our darkening world there is also much to say for Hardy's purity of mind and antique simplicity of art. There may also be something to say for his charity. Less austere and less ambitious than Conrad, Hardy confined himself to our unregenerate longing for happiness and our common destiny of suffering.

THE ILLUSION OF SIMPLICITY

The Poetry of Thomas Hardy

IT IS COMMON ENOUGH FOR READERS TO express a mild and casual preference for the poetry over the novels; or, at least, to cite Hardy's own distinct preference. The prose was "commercial," though rather less so than Hardy thought. But the poetry was cherished, incorruptible, and private, a form kept "alive from his early years, half in secrecy." The comment, nominally that of the second Mrs. Hardy, is presumably Hardy's own. Certainly the poetry was more varied and more experimental than the prose, less marred by sentimentality, and in divers ways more modern. And yet the body of criticism devoted to it is disproportionately small; and, so far as technique is concerned, very slight. Delmore Schwartz and W. H. Auden have written movingly of their personal responses to Hardy's poems. Samuel Hynes, Jr., David Perkins, and others have analyzed admirably recurrent preoccupations and themes. But the kind of intense scrutiny given Eliot, Pound, Yeats, and even Auden has been lacking. Presumably something about Hardy's poetry—perhaps its peculiar blend of plainness and eccentricity, perhaps the uninhibited directness of its sad and tired wisdom, perhaps the surface simplicity—disarms the critic. Much modern criticism consists of the elucidation of mysteries. But the interpreter is left with little to do where the poem's manifest meaning is so often the real one.

The major question remains, nevertheless, as it did for the novelist. Why does this "simple" poetry, with its transparency of statement and shameless reiteration, have such a considerable appeal for readers bred on ambiguity and paradox? One is thrown back, at the outset, on the large embarrassing categories of nineteenth-century criticism. First: this poetry achieves, to an exceptional degree, the pure, authentic, unpretentious, and precise expression of strong but uncomplicated emotion. The accent of total sincerity may not be the highest of poetic qualities, but it is a relatively rare one. This accent is absent from most of Hardy's war poems, as it is absent from nearly everyone's war poems; a factitious personality, borrowed unwittingly from editorials and from the "spirit of the time," speaks in place of an authentic self. And the accent of unmasked sincerity is also, I think, absent from Hardy's more abstract statements of fatalism. Here the poet was fulfilling a public and editorial role, even though it was a role frequently disclaimed. But in the poems not devoted to such themes —in the best lyrics, that is; in the poems of love and deprivation and mourning—the art of communication seems on the one hand private or intimate; and on the other hand, total. It is private and intimate in the sense that Hardy seems to speak very clearly but only to himself, or only to a single reader, whereas most nineteenth-century poets speak as though to a large public, more or less authoritatively. This is obviously true of Wordsworth and Tennyson. Speaking as to a large public normally involves some falsification of tone, some shifting of the poetic persona.* We have the sense with Hardy that the poetry has been little modified by the implicit existence of readers, or by the likelihood of publication. Many of Hardy's early poems went long unpublished; some were saved for the very last volumes in the 1920's.

If the act of communication in Hardy's best poems is intimate, it is also to a remarkable degree lucid and successful. The poems seem to express the feelings they want to express. The communication is not partial, blurred, or evasive. We do not get the sense of a baffled failure to communicate one feeling involving, by happy accident, the successful discovery of another. Hardy's lyric poetry, much more than his fiction, seems to realize its intentions.

And here again (as one looks from Hardy the poet to Hardy the novelist and Hardy the citizen) the success may seem surprising. For Hardy kept his personal experiences and even some of his strongest feelings out of his fiction to an extraordinary degree. Thus it takes a quasi-psychiatric criticism to discern, beneath the surface schemes of the novels, what the novelist's real sympathies and commitments were. Some of Hardy's most intense concerns *were closed off* from his fictional imagination; and many readers, loving Hardy's old-fashioned storytelling, will not regret this fact. Mrs. Hardy remarks that "there is more autobiography in a hundred lines of Mr. Hardy's poetry than in all of his novels." It is apparent that some of Hardy's most intense concerns and feelings were also closed off from his daily communication with his friends and with his first wife. This shy quiet man could not easily cross the ordinary barriers of personality. The failure of communication with his first wife was fairly sharp in the last year of her life. Yet shortly after her death he wrote more productively than ever before, and some of the poems of 1912-1913 are

*I do not refer to the normal shift which occurs as the citizen, sitting down to write, becomes a slightly different person. The successful writing of a "gloomy" poem could put Hardy in high spirits, as the official biography notes.

wholly successful evocations of his early love, of the Cornish romance of so many years before. Emotion repressed or suppressed or undiscovered both in the fiction and in life found, in the poetry, a fairly uninhibited and fairly precise expression.

A rare accent of sincerity, then, and a sense of expression fully realized—these are initial grounds for the poems' appeal. But the emotions themselves, and the long chronicle of bitter experience, are congenial. What irritated the late Victorians is pleasing to us, who prefer *Jude the Obscure* to *The Trumpet-Major*—the pure unsentimental notes of sadness, loneliness, and deprivation sounded decade after decade; the sense of life as a succession of small undramatic defeats; the honest declarations of unfaith and "unhope." There is a very modern awareness of psychic fatigue, of tiredness and dullness of spirit. And there is also, of course, the ironic awareness of ordinary human incompatibilities, of misplaced hopes and absurdly "mismatched destinies." These gray preoccupations may seem truer to our experience than the large dramatic aspirations and despairs of most nineteenth-century poetry; and truer also, it may be, than the neurotic alienation and utter psychic disruption conveyed by much poetry of the twentieth. Hardy's poetry, in other words—though it is limited, modest, and excludes a great deal of life—seems a true and therefore moving rendering of much intimate personal experience; and a wise measuring of it.

The "spoken" quality of the verse is a third ground for its modern appeal—the broken rhythms that follow the natural movements of voice, the quiet pace that refuses to be hurried by the meter, the sudden colloquial disruptions of metrical or stanzaic pattern, indeed all the various "antipoetic" twists and turns of a deliberately roughened art. This side of Hardy's poetry, though obvious, has had little attention. The official biography remarks that Hardy "had decided too regular a beat was bad art," and it emphasizes "the 'unforeseen' (as it has been called) character of his metres and stanzas, that of stress rather than of syllable, poetic texture rather than poetic veneer . . ." Hardy's respect for the rhythms of speech, and his usual repudiation of easy euphonies, place him with the early Wordsworth, with the Coleridge of the "Conversation Poems," with at least one of the Brownings and one of the Merediths. But the matter is more complex in Hardy than in any of them, since he did more conscious experimenting with meter. A peculiar source of roughness lies in the use of unfamiliar meters, and in a real ambiguity, at times, as to a poem's metrical norm. Hardy strove for the purely colloquial, and subordinated line to spoken phrase. But also he was a musician interested in sound patterns as such, in variation for its own sake. He even created verse-skeletons left blank or, occasionally, made up of nonsense verses. There were, we are told, "outlines and experiments in innumerable original measures."

One further and very important aspect of the art remains to be mentioned. It has been generally overlooked, yet is probably more responsible than anything else for the tension, strain, and paradox, the strangeness, that we have come to expect from modern poetry . . . and that do indeed exist in Hardy. This is his queer, "unforeseen," and even ironic use of poetic form, including both stanza and meter. A peculiar effect may derive, for instance, from a sharp discrepancy between nominal feeling and surface form; between very plain diction and highly ornamented stanza or elaborate meter; between simple gravity of theme and a form intrinsically light or even "playful." At an extreme a tragic or at least sad perception may be expressed in a triolet or other form of *vers de société*. The form thus comments on or modifies the stated emotion, and ends by rendering it more complex. Wordsworth, in "Peter Bell" and "The Idiot Boy," pushed the discrepancy between theme and meter to macabre extremes. But English verse and modern literature and art generally are rich in ironic uses of form. Examples at once come to mind, from the Elizabethan song or madrigal concerned with death or tragic separation, or from classical French tragedy with its sprightly stylizations of the most sombre declarations . . . to the conversion of Leopold Bloom's spiritual torment to comic expressionist fantasy. The reduction of history and suffering to anecdote, the comic distortions of violence, all the innumerable stylizations of grief, the blunted obtuse responses of a fictional narrator to the tragic story he tells, the framing of tragic statement (in any art form) by playful decoration . . . these are all modes of psychic distancing that affect, distort, modify meanings, and often enrich or illumine them.

This ironic use of form is, in any event, a central element of Hardy's appeal.

We may take a very early poem and a very late one, written fifty-three years apart, to suggest some of Hardy's important peculiarities. (These are not, it should be noted, characteristically early and late; the poetry changed little from decade to decade.)

NEUTRAL TONES

We stood by a pond that winter day,
And the sun was white, as though chidden of God,
And a few leaves lay on the starving sod;
  —They had fallen from an ash, and were gray.

Your eyes on me were as eyes that rove
Over tedious riddles of years ago;
And some words played between us to and fro
  On which lost the more by our love.

The smile on your mouth was the deadest thing
Alive enough to have strength to die;
And a grin of bitterness swept thereby
  Like an ominous bird a-wing. . . .

Since then, keen lessons that love deceives,
And wrings with wrong, have shaped to me
Your face, and the God-curst sun, and a tree,
  And a pond edged with grayish leaves.

(1867)

"IF YOU HAD KNOWN"

If you had known
When listening with her to the far-down moan
Of the white-selvaged and empurpled sea,
And rain came on that did not hinder talk,
Or damp your flashing facile gaiety
In turning home, despite the slow wet walk
By crooked ways, and over stiles of stone;
  If you had known

You would lay roses,
Fifty years thence, on her monument, that discloses
Its graying shape upon the luxuriant green;
Fifty years thence to an hour, by chance led there,
What might have moved you?—yea, had you foreseen
That on the tomb of the selfsame one, gone where
The dawn of every day is as the close is,
  You would lay roses!

(1920)

The early poem is the better of the two, as well as the more modern in its craggy plainness. Yet these very different poems were unmistakably written by the same hand, and exhibit some of the same oddities. Both poems are concerned with an ironic contrast of the knowledgeable present and the innocent unknowing past. The situation is more dramatic in "Neutral Tones." "Neutral Tones," moreover, purports to be a direct, matter-of-fact, stolid rendering of the speaker's experience; it is written in "neutral tones." Realism prevails over the brief temptation to be literary and decorative. The sun is white, "as though chidden of God"—a trivial matter, since a chiding threatens no one. And in the third stanza the "ominous bird a-wing" may, as a romantic cliché, take away some of the grin's bitterness. But these are inadequacies of the speaker (who has not yet had his "keen lessons"), not of the poem. He can observe but not understand how weary the loved one is, how tedious these riddles are. By the fourth stanza, however, he has achieved her understanding. Now the chidden sun has become a God-curst sun. And in place of harmless simile we have that terrible immobility of the remembered scene:

> Your face, and the God-curst sun, and a tree,
> And a pond edged with grayish leaves.

The theme of " 'If You Had Known' " is an obvious one, but it is also a theme of almost obsessive importance for Hardy—failure to anticipate the loved one's death and so failure to act appropriately while she was still alive. We are compelled to recall again the coolness and diffidence of Hardy's relationship with his first wife, just prior to her death, and his subsequent feelings of guilt. In that context the statement that the lover would have laid roses, had he known, may not be as slight a one as it seems at first. But even without biography we see that the poem's appeal lies in the conflict between a seriousness of feeling (conveyed by the colloquial realism and spoken rhythms of lines 4, 6-7, 10, 12, 14) and a decorative, conventional stanza (the refrains, of course, but also the rhyme play of *discloses, close is, roses*). There is a literary formalizing of grief. The speaker seems to protect himself, through the decorativeness, from too intimate and too intense an involvement.

The style of "Neutral Tones" is indeed plain and matter-of-fact. The details are enumerated, and there is a conspicuous refusal to seek striking analogy:

> The smile on your mouth was the deadest thing
> Alive enough to have strength to die . . .

This is the honest observation of a speaker incapable of simile or original metaphor. In the fourth stanza a considerable intensification is achieved, through compression, but the language remains simple and, in fact, monosyllabic. The language of " 'If You Had Known' " is distinctly more literary, but the old plainness is there in lines 4, 6, 7, 10, 12. In both poems normal and even relaxed speech rhythms, rhythms very close to those of prose, combat the demands of meter and line length, and in fact prevail over them. The speaker refuses to be hurried; and in lines 5 and 6 of " 'If You Had Known' " the phrase seems to have no relationship at all to the line.

And it is here that the two poems are most alike and most characteristic: in their refusal to permit an easy correspondence of spoken phrase and written line. This is a common source of Hardy's roughness. The reader who respects the speech rhythms of the phrase repeatedly finds himself in awkward metrical situations. The resulting tension is one of several reasons why the "simple" Hardy is not so simple after all. (It should be noted again that this roughness is deliberate. "Her Dilemma," written in 1866, though it exploits pleasing speech rhythms, has an absolute metrical regularity. The last stanza of "Beeny Cliff," modeled after Poe, shows, even in the difficult fifteen-syllable line, an almost Poesque regularity.)

To account for the characteristic Hardy roughness, we must look at meter. "Neutral Tones" is typically deceptive. At a glance, and before any attempt has been made to read it aloud, this would seem to be a normal accentual-syllabic* poem with all but one of the long lines of either nine or

---

*In accentual-syllabic poetry there is a predetermined number of accented and unaccented syllables, normally divided into feet. Accent is determined by pitch. In accentual poetry, where accent is determined by speech stress, the number of syllables is not predetermined.

ten syllables. The one eight-syllable line is regularly iambic: the division into feet could not be more pronounced. But of course a nine-syllable variation on a five-accent, ten-syllable line is very far from normal. And if we pursue the matter further (still seeking an accentual-syllabic norm) we find a fairly large number of inverted feet, twenty-four in sixteen lines. The baffled reader may then decide—even though there is so little variety in line length—that he is faced with a poem in accentual meter. But here too one's expectations (now of a four-stress line) are violated by, at least, the third, seventh, thirteenth, and fifteenth lines. To sum up: colloquial, prosy speech rhythm not only moves in counterpoint to the metrical line. The metrical line itself oscillates between the strict accentual-syllabic norm and the looser accentual. In a word, Hardy will not permit the reader to settle comfortably into a familiar gait.

The metrical situation in "'If You Had Known'" is somewhat less complicated. In the first stanza we are clearly dealing with a five-accent, ten-syllable accentual-syllabic line, even though the collision of phrase and line is fairly sharp in lines 5, 6, and 7. But in lines 2 and 3 Hardy is exploiting some of the classic and beautiful variations possible in an accentual-syllabic line, especially variety of degree of accent:

> When listening with her to the far-down moan
> Of the white-selvaged and empurpled sea . . .

The second stanza is a much less innocent affair, and we find that only the next-to-last line is metrically regular, though it adds a feminine ending. Lines 10 through 14 are strange. Line 10, for instance,

> Fifty/years thence,/on her mon/*u*ment, that/discloses

offers the following variations on the norm: inverted first foot, strong unaccented syllable in the second foot, trisyllabic substitution in the third foot, elision of the first syllable in the fourth foot, feminine ending added to the fifth foot.

These technical considerations, however wearisome to the reader of a critique of the poetry, cannot be omitted, if we want to account for a full, alert response to the poetry. A very large number of Hardy's poems, if similarly analyzed, would surrender similar complexities and uncertainties of rhythm and meter.

To read the collected poems of Hardy in sequence is a very different experience from that of reading Wordsworth's. Hardy is certainly uneven and there are comparatively few poems worth retaining from his last three collections, all published in the 1920's. (The three volumes occupy 355 of 887 pages in the *Collected Poems.*) But the unevenness existed from the first. There was never a sharp anti-climax; nothing at all comparable to Wordsworth's hysteria of 1812 and 1813, or to the solemnity, literalism, and frequent silliness of his last thirty years. ("The Birdcatcher's Boy" of 1912 comes closest to the silliness of the late Wordsworth.) Had Hardy classified his poems in a way that concealed chronology, as Wordsworth did, our view of him would hardly be changed. The voice of "Neutral Tones" may be heard in very late poems. But not only the voice. What is truly extraordinary is to hear the same notes of mourning and melancholia, of deprivation and nostalgia, struck volume after volume, decade after decade.

It may be useful to establish a few categories, and to dismiss briefly the minor ones. The number of occasional and incidental poems, poems of experience dutifully observed and noted down, is very large in Wordsworth. In Hardy it is relatively small. We have a few poems presumably influenced by Wordsworth—"The Widow Betrothed" and "The Workbox," for instance, poems of rural mischance in the jingly *Lyrical Ballads* measure. "At a Country Fair," in which the speaker reports seeing a giant led by a dwarf on a string, records the kind of "episode" Wordsworth would not, humorlessly, have missed. The conclusion almost reads like parody of Wordsworth:

> Various sights in various climes
> I have seen, and more I may see yet,
> But that sight never shall I forget,
> And have thought it the sorriest of pantomimes,
> If once, a hundred times!

At a quite different level the fine consecrative poem "Drummer Hodge" bears some relationship to "A Slumber Did My Spirit Seal," with its evocation of the turning earth. The poem is saved from cliché by its stately measure, and by the distancing insistence on "foreign constellations," "strange stars," and "strange-eyed constellations." One fine short poem of Landorian perfection also had its nominal origin in war: "In Time of 'The Breaking of Nations'." Again, to take another kind of nineteenth-century "set piece," Hardy exploits romantic literary associations in "Shelley's Skylark" and "At the Pyramid of Cestius: Near the Graves of Shelley and Keats." The two poems are by no means bad; they have the peculiar Hardy merit of saying something not very complex exactly as it was intended to be said.

An important though small category is that of the true ballad poems and "ballad-tragedies." (Hardy called "The Sacrilege" a ballad-tragedy, and it is a good term for poems giving more circumstantial detail than the traditional ballads do.) With these belong the poems exploiting Wessex traditions. "The Bride-Night Fire" of 1866, written in dialect, shows how early this impulse was. "The Tree," "The Lost Pyx," "A Sunday Morning Tragedy," and "The Flirt's Tragedy" are fine traditional narratives. In "The Vampirine Fair" the pure ballad directness is combined with the dramatic monologue's interest in self-characterization and self-betrayal. But the great poem in the ballad-tragedy mode is "A Trampwoman's Tragedy," an utterly realistic first-person narrative of perversity and retribution —a perversity stemming in part from weariness, as in life it so often does, weariness and boredom. Hardy considered this in some ways his most successful poem. The authentic voice and humble verisimilar detail, and the immediacy of the dramatic action, play ironically against both the conventional poetic pattern (involving two triplets) and an occasional romantic rendering of landscape. The short second line, picking up the end of the first, conveys the weariness—weariness of the flesh and of the spirit—that seems to be at the heart of the poem, a weariness present even at the moment of murder:

> From Wynyard's Gap the livelong day,
>   The livelong day,
> We beat afoot the northward way
>   We had travelled times before.
> The sun-blaze burning on our backs,
> Our shoulders sticking to our packs,
> By fosseway, fields, and turnpike tracks
>   We skirted sad Sedge-Moor. (I)
>
> . . . .
>
> Then up he sprung, and with his knife—
>   And with his knife
> He let out jeering Johnny's life,
>   Yes; there, at set of sun.
> The slant ray through the window nigh
> Gilded John's blood and glazing eye,
> Ere scarcely Mother Lee and I
>   Knew that the deed was done. (IX)

Related to the ballad poems and historical narratives are a number of personal lyrics evoking the "dark backward" of the Wessex past. "The Roman Road," juxtaposing helmed legionaries and a mother's form, is a beautifully compact poem of this kind. "Channel Firing," a famous and perhaps overpraised poem, conveys this sense of time rather theoretically. In "A Wet Night" the speaker evokes forebears whose struggles and discomforts were much greater than his own. These poems reflect an important aspect of Hardy's temperament and mentality. The "now" and "then" are often ironically juxtaposed, in the poetry, but the memorial impulses and local pieties are genuine. This is the Hardy of the novels and of *The Dynasts,* for whom the past is hauntingly alive. It is pleasing to find such a poem as "The Clasped Skeletons" in the posthumous volume—the skeletons uncovered in "an Ancient British barrow near the writer's house": "Surmised Date 1800 B.C." These had antedated a number of historical lovers who are wittily enumerated:

> Aye, even before the beauteous Jael
>   Bade Sisera doff his gear
> And lie in her tent; then drove the nail,
>   You two lay here.
>
> Wicked Aholah, in her youth,
>   Colled loves from far and near
> Until they slew her without ruth;
>   But you had long colled here.
>
> Aspasia lay with Pericles,
>   And Philip's son found cheer
> At eves in lying on Thais' knees
>   While you lay here.
>
> Cleopatra with Antony,
>   Resigned to dalliance sheer,
> Lay, fatuous he, insatiate she,
>   Long after you'd lain here . . .

One further historical poem may be mentioned: "Panthera," a dramatic monologue and historical reconstruction in the manner of Browning, but with less eccentricity and with a calmer realism than Browning usually shows. Hardy here applies the quiet blank verse of the "Conversation Poem" to a melodramatic situation. In the weakness of the fifth foot Hardy has moved very far toward the conversational blank verse of, for instance, Frost:

> . . . "A tedious time
> I found it, of routine, amid a folk
> Restless, contentless, and irascible.—
> Quelling some riot, sentrying court and hall,
> Sending men forth on public meeting-days
> To maintain order, were my duties there.
>
> . . . .
>
> I, mounted on a Cappadocian horse,
> With some half-company of auxiliaries,
> Had captained the procession through the streets
> When it came streaming from the judgment-hall
> After the verdicts of the Governor."

The abstract and even pedantic pessimism that occasionally mars Hardy's novels, the dogged schematizings of gloom, appears notoriously in a number of poems. "Hap" at the very outset (1866) speaks of "Crass Casualty" and "purblind Doomsters," but not even *The Dynasts,* so many years later, could exhaust Hardy's impulse to systematize bad luck. "Doom and She," a tendentious colloquy between the "world weaver" and a shadowy companion, is one of a number of tiresome debates. In "By the Earth's Corpse," a conversation occurring after all life on earth has ended, the Lord repents of having made earth, life, and man. The abstract pessimism is particularly disagreeable where expressed in very long lines, as in "The Lacking Sense." The melodramatic "Convergence of the Twain" (of the *Titanic* and the iceberg) has some fine lines, and it has at least the virtue of dramatizing the fatalism succinctly.

Hardy's temperamental gloom, when not snared in such abstractions, is another matter. Some of the finest poems are too familiar to require analysis. The nostalgia for lost faith in "The Oxen," the beautiful "neutral tones" of "The Darkling Thrush," the extraordinarily compressed rationale of "unhope" in the first of the *In Tenebris* poems—these convey not a theory of causality but a mature human temperament, scored by disillusioned wisdom. Few poets, moreover, perhaps none, have conveyed as persuasively as Hardy a dullness of spirit—not Baudelaire's ennui, not extreme dryness or despair, not a pathological acedia, but a sense of slack indifference, an undramatic nothingness.

These are, in Hardy's verse, the secondary categories and impulses. By all odds his most authentic note is that of *mourning*: mourning over the dead, over the death of love, over the death of the heart. Of the hundreds of poems of love, one ("Under a Waterfall") may be described as relatively happy, though it too deals with a "now" and "then." Plunging his arms into the water where a cup, once shared with the loved one, had been dropped by accident, and which is still there, the speaker experiences a Proustian recovery of the past. Moreover the famous poems of 1912-1913, written immediately after his first wife's death, are not all sad. In reality several assert the triumph of memory, and of a qualitatively immortal experience, over time and death. In "A Dream Or No," "At Castle Boterel," and "Beeny Cliff" the past is by no means dead, nor is it ironically discredited.

The remainder of the love poems, and poems of loneliness and deprivation and regret, constitute one of the purest, least pretentious, and saddest bodies of writing in English. Many of these poems are concerned with quiet almost imponderable failures, the undramatic quotidian failures that scar love and exhaust the heart. They are concerned with "failures of communication"; or, as Forster puts it, failures to "connect." One loves inadequately, inappropriately, or at the wrong time; or one fails to make amends. These are poems of marriage and of mature lovers, or of older persons looking far back on youthful ardor. Hardy's love poems convey no dissolvings of personality and wild escapes of the heart. The note of calm weariness is rarely absent. In "Side by Side" (to take an extreme example) an estranged couple chance to sit side by side in church, and so are thought to be reconciled. They agree not to undeceive their friends. But that is their only reunion; they separate at the door of the church "To meet no more / In their span of days." A chance meeting that led to nothing, where so many meetings are missed that might have changed the lovers' lives! Poems of mischance these are, but also poems of ordinary human failure, which is not a matter of chance. The speaker cannot know that his former sweetheart lies dying in a house opposite, to whom he might have brought happiness at the end ("At Mayfair Lodgings"). This is a mischance and irony worthy of one of Hardy's short stories. But the original tragedy now ending need not have occurred, we learn, "Had she been less unbending." However, revisitations may also prove ironically misguided, and our fidelities absurd. The loved one we look up may turn out to be degenerate or grotesquely aged ("My Cicely," "The Revisitation").

There are a number of poems conveying ordinary nostalgia for lost youth and half-forgotten pleasures; there are the "Reminiscences of a Dancing Man." (The half-forgetting is itself a betrayal.) It is the heart not the flesh that dies, as a rule, in this poetry. "I looked into my glass" conveys the contrary experience of vivid emotion and desire in an aged body: still another form of isolation. A number of poems deal fairly directly with the experience of the man who survives to old age, and observes the successive deaths of friends, as in "The Five Students." "During Wind and Rain," in which the speaker seems to stand outside time, shuttling between the "then" and the "now," underscores dramatically, in the long, thick last lines of each stanza, the poignancy of survival. To capture the past, and to fail to capture it, alike define a solitude, as Proust too recognized.

This note of separateness, that the two lovers remain two, is one of Hardy's insistences. "Only connect . . ." There is—surprisingly successful in "My spirit will not haunt the mound," "'Something Tapped'," and "The Shadow on the Stone"—the fantasy of communication with the dead; or of attempted communication, on the part of the dead one, that has failed. The experience is presented realistically, as an actual illusion. But it is also a paradigm of a failure to respond to overtures. Related to it is the major irony of loving intensely, after death, one not adequately loved when alive. "An Upbraiding" asks whether the surviving lover who now sings songs to her will return, when he too is dead and with her, to his erstwhile coldness. The question with its added irony (since the lover will indeed be cold) surely has some bearing on the 1912-1913 love poems. Hardy seems to have been quite aware that he was living, in this sudden renascence of love, and in the beautiful poems which ensued, one of his own characteristic inventions, an irony of belated fidelity.

Innumerable poems in various languages celebrate the transfiguring effect of love. Hardy dramatizes also the transfiguring force of love's death or decline. The outward world has changed back to its real form, or has become drabber than nature. An important variant on the classic invocations to intensity of feeling is the plea, in several moving poems, for unfeeling, the security of the numbed heart. This impulse (which was very important but largely unconscious in Wordsworth) was conscious enough in Hardy. "Revulsion" is unique in its misogyny or sexual fear, and the poem is overly explicit. The usual fear is one of deprivation, disillusionment . . . or of a memory too vivid. In "Shut Out That Moon" the speaker shies away from associations evoking a time when illusions remained. The methodical, even-paced progress of the poem has the quality of incantation, but incantation designed to put the heart to sleep:

> Within the common lamp-lit room
> Prison my eyes and thought;
> Let dingy details crudely loom,
> Mechanic speech be wrought . . .

The loved one of "In a Cathedral City," whether dead or not, is lost. Here too the speaker seeks a "formal feeling," the protection of coldness. This is not merely the subject of the poem, but reflects its rigorously ordered, logical method:

> These people have not heard your name;
> No loungers in this placid place
> Have helped to bruit your beauty's fame.
>
> The grey Cathedral, towards whose face
> Bend eyes untold, has met not yours;
> Your shade has never swept its base,
>
> Your form has never darked its doors,
> Nor have your faultless feet once thrown
> A pensive pit-pat on its floors.
>
> Along the street to maids well known
> Blithe lovers hum their tender airs,
> But in your praise voice not a tone. . . .
>
> —Since nought bespeaks you here, or bears,
> As I, your imprint through and through,
> Here might I rest, till my heart shares
> The spot's unconsciousness of you!

Some of the most successful poems dramatize moments of vision and intuition, particular incidents in the growth and death of love. These are essentially dramatic poems. In "Honeymoon Time at an Inn" there is sadness in the hour of felicity, and an intuition of future unhappiness—

a significant and not unusual reaction, yet one that rarely finds its way into poetry. The converse, as poignant and perhaps as common in life, evokes the momentary recovery, many years after "age has scared romance," of a youthful love. Thus the well-known "A Church Romance." The sonnet exhibits the extraordinary compression of which Hardy was capable, and his ability to keep calm and unhurried a poem narrating so much in fourteen lines:

> She turned in the high pew, until her sight
> Swept the west gallery, and caught its row
> Of music-men with viol, book, and bow
> Against the sinking sad tower-window light.
>
> She turned again; and in her pride's despite
> One strenuous viol's inspirer seemed to throw
> A message from his string to her below,
> Which said: "I claim thee as my own forthright!"
>
> Thus their hearts' bond began, in due time signed.
> And long years thence, when Age had scared Romance,
> At some old attitude of his or glance
> That gallery-scene would break upon her mind,
> With him as minstrel, ardent, young, and trim,
> Bowing "New Sabbath" or "Mount Ephraim."

Even more representative of Hardy's sadness, or providing at least an area of feeling no other English poet has realized as well, is the bitter recognition that love not merely dies but becomes "tedious," though not at the same rate for both lovers. More representative, in other words, is "Neutral Tones." In most English poetry lovers rarely remain together after love has slackened or died; in Hardy's poetry, as in life, they do. "Near Lanivet, 1872" is a highly successful poem dealing with this very particular sadness, and with the irony implicit in discrepancies of feeling, in different degrees of slackened love. *Post coitum . . . animal triste* is an experience conveyed by a number of poets since Donne. But this drabber and more durable sadness is particularly Hardy's. Once again the deliberateness of the pace, the careful composition of the scene, the precise unhurried structuring of feeling, seem acts both of responsible, faithful remembering, and of self-protective ordering. Nothing is forgotten, and nothing escapes emotional control.

There was a stunted handpost just on the crest,
    Only a few feet high:
She was tired, and we stopped in the twilight-time
        for her rest,
    At the crossways close thereby.

She leant back, being so weary, against its stem,
    And laid her arms on its own,
Each open palm stretched out to each end of them,
    Her sad face sideways thrown.

Her white-clothed form at this dim-lit cease of day
    Made her look as one crucified
In my gaze at her from the midst of the dusty way,
    And hurriedly "Don't," I cried.

I do not think she heard. Loosing thence she said,
    As she stepped forth ready to go,
"I am rested now.—Something strange came into
        my head;
    I wish I had not leant so!"

And wordless we moved onward down from the
        hill
    In the west cloud's murked obscure,
And looking back we could see the handpost still
    In the solitude of the moor.

"It struck her too," I thought, for as if afraid
  She heavily breathed as we trailed;

Till she said, "I did not think how 'twould look
in the shade,
When I leant there like one nailed."

I, lightly: "There's nothing in it. For *you,*
anyhow!"
—"O I know there is not," said she . . .
"Yet I wonder . . . If no one is bodily crucified
now,
In spirit one may be!"

And we dragged on and on, while we seemed to see
In the running of Time's far glass
Her crucified, as she had wondered if she might be
Some day.—Alas, alas!

Much attention has been given to Hardy's temperamental gloom, some to his diction, but little to his formal and metrical experiments. There are, to recapitulate, the two impulses in Hardy's poetry. The first is anti-poetic and conversational. It strives for a colloquial, realistic, unhurried, even prosy voice, a voice of many dissonances and cacophonies. This is a style of broken rhythms and often harsh phrasing consciously opposed to the lulling liquid euphonies of Shelley, Tennyson, Swinburne. Some of Hardy's critics (like some of Landor's) have assumed this roughness was undeliberate. But a considerable number of obviously graceful poems shows this to be untrue.

The second major impulse is formalistic, and reflects both an acchitect's interest in patterns and a musician's interest in new meters and odd rhythms. This is the Hardy of the verse skeletons and nonsense verses, the Hardy who tried out such a large number of verse forms, the Hardy who (in "The Respectable Burgher") wrote a thirty-six-line poem on a single rhyme.

There are, we have seen, important relationships between the two impulses in Hardy's poetry. On the one hand, some of the metrical experiments are designed to bring out colloquial rhythms and dissonances, especially the experiments with long lines. On the other hand, there sometimes exists an ironic counterpoint between gravity of feeling and a playful intricacy of stanza and meter. Here we find, once again, the ironic use of form that is one of Hardy's important strangenesses.

The obvious medium for expressing the speaking voice realistically is the unpretentious but carefully modulated blank verse of "Panthera"—the familiar blank verse of a quiet "Conversation Poem." Here many lovely variations are possible, and, especially, great varieties in degree of accent, within a perfectly recognizable norm. But Hardy also tried for colloquial naturalness in a number of unusual meters, some of which refuse to recognize any norm. "Honeymoon Time at an Inn," to take an extreme example, is almost ruthlessly experimental. This is one of a number of Hardy poems, of deceptively familiar appearance on the printed page, which prove on close examination to be metrically very strange.

The look of this poem is wholly reassuring. We have eight stanzas, with the first, third, fourth, and fifth lines of each stanza fairly long, and the second and sixth lines short. There is every reason to expect an accentual-syllabic poem of considerable regularity. But the poem, so long as we preserve these expectations, simply cannot be read; the ear is perpetually baffled. If we scan the poem, looking for the sources of bafflement, we find that the "long" lines vary from ten to fifteen syllables and the "short" ones from six to eight. If we now look instead for a purely accentual norm based on true speech stresses, we find that the long lines run from four accents to seven and the short lines from three to four. These variations, though marked, are less extreme than in a number of poems that present less difficulty. If we look at our scansion again, our verse-skeleton, and note also the quantitatively strong unaccented syllables (one of the most important variations in English verse), and note of course the inversions of accent, we find something truly astonishing. The fifth line of the first stanza repeats the first line. This occurs again, with a slight change in wording, in the seventh stanza. This leaves us with a theoretical possibility, for a forty-eight-line poem, of forty-six different types of metrical line. *And this is precisely what we have!* Except for the lines noted above, no two are rhythmically alike. Granted the principle of monotony implicit in perpetual variety, such extreme variation is no mean tour de force. It is interesting to note that Hardy made this extreme experiment in a serious and ambitious poem.

Hardy experimented early and late with very long lines, and used a number of times the queer fifteen-syllable, eight-accent form. These poems, though not very successful, represent serious efforts both to find a new music and to catch the rhythms of a speaking voice. A full study of Hardy's versification—and of his colloquial roughness—would need to consider these, and to consider as well his experiments in quantitative verse.

The counterpoint of simplicity and seriousness of theme and elaborate, decorative, or playful form—the ironic use of form, that is—appears in a very large number of poems. The odd juxtaposition of sombre feeling and sprightly stanza occurs from first to last; it is present in most of the many poems having abrupt shifts from long to very short lines. The purest type of ironic form would be that of *vers de société* used to express suffering: for instance, the triolet begining "How great my grief, my joys how few." But such a poem never really asks to be taken seriously. It is more relevant to take, as example, a serious, successful, and even complex poem, and one which derives part of its meaning from the subtle relationship of stated feeling and stanza, rhyme, meter. "'I Found Her Out There'" is one of the 1912-1913 poems written shortly after the first Mrs. Hardy's death:

I found her out there
On a slope few see,
That falls westwardly
To the salt-edged air,
Where the ocean breaks
On the purple strand,
And the hurricane shakes
The solid land.

I brought her here,
And have laid her to rest
In a noiseless nest
No sea beats near.
She will never be stirred
In her loamy cell
By the waves long heard
And loved so well.

So she does not sleep
By those haunted heights
The Atlantic smites
And the blind gales sweep,
Whence she often would gaze
At Dundagel's famed head,
While the dipping blaze
Dyed her face fire-red;

And would sigh at the tale
Of sunk Lyonnesse,
As a wind-tugged tress
Flapped her cheek like a flail;
Or listen at whiles
With a thought-bound brow
To the murmuring miles
She is far from now.

Yet her shade, maybe,
Will creep underground
Till it catch the sound
Of that western sea
As it swells and sobs
Where she once domiciled,
And joy in its throbs
With the heart of a child.

Some readers might recognize at once the seriousness of this poem, and discount the apparent playfulness of the first two stanzas—the lightness implicit in the short lines and in the fanciful "nest" and "loamy cell." I am not sure. I think it would be more natural for the reader (remembering the dry sincerities of "Neutral Tones" and "Near Lanivet") to observe the oddity of such a very detached and literary treatment of the burial of a loved one. Or he might expect a purely formal exercise similar to "How great my grief, my joys how few." For one thing the unusual and lovely meter, with its subtle variations, calls attention to itself. The first four lines of the first two stanzas, these eight lines in fact, are metrically different; there is a very delicate interplay of voice and meter. The language too suggests a commemorative but not intimate poem. A loved one has been buried away from the sea, but this loved one is only "her"; she has been brought to a vague "here," away from a "there" of disturbing hurricanes and beating seas. She has been depersonalized, dehumanized even, so that she occupies a "noiseless nest" and a "loamy cell." Only the last line of the second stanza suggests she might have preferred to be buried "out there," and this preference begins to give her some real existence.

The third and fourth stanzas (with their slightly longer and less playful lines) bring a sharp reversal. The forsaken sea has "haunted heights"; it has "Dundagel's famed head"; it embraces "sunk Lyonnesse"; its "murmuring miles" induce thought. And as the menacing sea is radically revalued, so the loved one associated with it is brought vividly to life: her face fire-red, and with hair flapping her cheeks like a flail. "Out there" she was wonderfully alive, and partook of nature's violence as well as its quietness. In brief, the innocuous fantasy of the first two stanzas has been replaced by vivid memory.

In the final stanza the speaker returns to his vein of fantasy, or tries to: perhaps her shade will creep underground, back to that loved western sea. But the achieved tone is now very different. For it had been a betrayal to bury her "here" rather than "out there," where she had once *domiciled.* There is a necessary irony and distancing —distancing too from the speaker—in the use of the abstract word. The words "once domiciled" throw us back to line nine: we realize the loved one had been brought "here" not merely for burial but for a large part of her life. And this is of course one meaning of this poem, which is indeed an intimate one: *it had been a betrayal to bring her "here" at all;* it had even been a betrayal to marry her. The poem's devaluation of *here* is by implication a devaluation of the speaker. The poem thus turns out to be far more personal and far more deeply committed than it seemed at first glance. As its underlying meaning and gravity emerge, and as we go back, we are likely to read the first stanzas more slowly than before. Yet the beauty intrinsic in ironic form, in a seeming "lightness" at variance with actual seriousness of theme, will continue to be felt.

Another 1912-1913 poem, "A Dream or No," has a familiar and related theme—failure of memory and so of the heart, the dislimning in memory of the loved one.

Why go to Saint-Juliot? What's Juliot to me?
    Some strange necromancy
    But charmed me to fancy
That much of my life claims the spot as its key.

Yes. I have had dreams of that place in the West,
And a maiden abiding
Thereat as in hiding;
Fair-eyed and white-shouldered, broad-browed and
brown-tressed

And of how, coastward bound on a night long ago,
There lonely I found her,
The sea-birds around her,
And other than nigh things uncaring to know.

So sweet her life there (in my thought has it seemed)
That quickly she drew me
To take her unto me,
And lodge her long years with me. Such have I dreamed.

But nought of that maid from Saint-Juliot I see;
Can she ever have been here,
And shed her life's sheen here,
The woman I thought a long housemate with me?

Does there even a place like Saint-Juliot exist?
Or a Vallency Valley
With stream and leafed alley,
Or Beeny, or Bos with its flounce flinging mist?

This time the speaker's early statements seem deceptive, rather than the meter. He suggests that having had a loved one in Saint-Juliot is only fantasy, but we know this is a pretense. So we seem confronted at the start with trivial and literary *données,* and the playful second and third lines reinforce this impression. In the second stanza the spot is vaguely "a place in the West," and the loved one is "a maiden" of stereotyped or dreamlike lineaments; again the short second and third lines are playful, as is the word "Thereat." The long, slow, colloquial ninth line begins to lend some reality to the woman, who is truly individualized in her solitude, with the sea-birds around her. Her attachment to nigh things is strongly accented by the aloof "uncaring to know." In the fourth stanza, with its colloquial turns and unpretentious repetition of *me,* the loved one's reality is firmly established. Of course such a person existed! But the memory of her remains abstract, the memory of a circumstance. In this stanza and in the next the short lines are no longer playful. The fifth stanza deals frankly with this failure of memory. How can anything really have existed which has left so little behind? The speaker never does make more concrete that later life with the "housemate." But his initial failure of memory dealt nominally with Saint-Juliot, and whether memory of finding the maiden could become real. Now the puzzled tones ask, in a prosy long line, whether "even a place like Saint-Juliot" exists. But that is the end of the prosiness. The last three lines, with their place names (two of these vividly characterized) answer in triumphantly musical lines. Paradoxically, real reality is at last conveyed not in colloquialisms but in highly euphonious lines. Memory in all its romantic reality is revived; the past has been recaptured.

These poems, and other love poems in the 1912-1913 series (notably "Beeny Cliff," "Places," and "The Phantom Horsewoman") are radically different in method from the sombre realistic "Neutral Tones" and "Near Lanivet" and the other love poems of spiritual fatigue. But how much wider is the difference between any one of these poems and "The Darkling Thrush," or between "The Darkling Thrush" and "A Trampwoman's Tragedy"! All this is only to suggest that Hardy, though he repeated himself a good deal, is a richer and more versatile poet than is commonly assumed. Yet behind the diverse subjects and multiplicity of experimented forms one nearly always hears the recognizable personal voice, the grave, sad, and unhurried voice with its accent of unmistakable sincerity—the mature expression, decade after decade, of an exceptionally pure and authentic temperament.

This deep, moving, and easily accessible humanity may be one of the reasons why criticism, in the presence of Hardy, has found itself disarmed; why it has not yet exposed him, that is, to the rigorous analysis lesser poets have received.

NOTES

Page references to Hardy's novels are to the Harper Thin-Paper Edition of 1910, unless otherwise indicated.

1. Florence Emily Hardy, *The Early Life of Thomas Hardy* (London, 1928), p. 110.

2. "Candour in English Fiction," *The New Review,* II (1890), 8. In the same issue and on the same subject Hardy wrote that the "crash of broken commandments is as necessary to the catastrophe of a tragedy as the noise of drums and cymbals to a triumphal march" (p. 18).

3. William R. Rutland, *Thomas Hardy: A Study of His Writings and Their Background* (Oxford, 1938), p. 187.

4. Katherine Anne Porter, "Notes on a Criticism of Thomas Hardy," Thomas Hardy Centennial Issue, *The Southern Review,* VI (Summer, 1940), p. 156.

5. Howard Baker, "Hardy's Poetic Certitude," *ibid.,* p. 54.

6. Samuel C. Chew, *Thomas Hardy: Poet and Novelist* (New York, 1928), p. 134. *The Mayor of Casterbridge* lacks "charm, sweetness, poetry" (p. 49).

7. Thomas Hardy, "The Profitable Reading of Fiction," *The Forum,* V (1888), 58, 65. See also *The Early Life of Thomas Hardy,* pp. 193, 194, 231, 232, 242, 299, and Florence Emily Hardy, *The Later Years of Thomas Hardy* (New York, 1930), p. 16.

8. See Donald Davidson's excellent "The Traditional Basis of Thomas Hardy's Fiction," *The Southern Review,* VI (Summer, 1940), 162-178. Ruth A. Firor's *Folkways in Thomas Hardy* (Philadelphia, 1931) is an exhaustive and learned but highly readable treatise not only on Hardy's use of folk material but on this folk material itself.

9. We do not have to agree with George Moore (who singled out this famous flight at the beginning of *The Return of the Native)* that Thomas

Hardy wrote the worst prose of the nineteenth century (*Conversations in Ebury Street* [New York, 1924], pp. 118, 140-143.) Temperament generally gets into and compensates for the doggedness of Hardy's prose structure and the heaviness with which he plans a major effect. The judgment of Katherine Anne Porter seems to me a fair one: "Who does not remember it? And in actual re-reading, what could be duller? What could be more labored than his introduction of the widow Yeobright at the heath fire among the dancers, or more unconvincing than the fears of the timid boy that the assembly are literally raising the Devil? Except for this: in my memory of that episode, as in dozens of others in many of Hardy's novels, I have seen it, I was there. When I read it, it almost disappears from view, and afterward comes back, phraseless, living in its sombre clearness, as Hardy meant it to do, I feel certain" (*The Southern Review,* VI [Summer, 1940], 161). As Havelock Ellis said, Hardy was without training as a literary artist: "It is genius that carries him through" (Introduction to Pierre d'Exideuil, *The Human Pair in the Work of Thomas Hardy* [London, n.d.], p. xv).

10. Lord David Cecil, *Hardy the Novelist: An Essay in Criticism* (New York, 1946), p. 218.

11. Lascelles Abercrombie's *Thomas Hardy: A Critical Study* (New York, 1912) is the best analysis of this "vision." See pp. 21, 25, 36, 102, 123, 136. But even this distinguished book overemphasizes the philosophical impulse. We must overlook Hardy's lifelong fascination with the Napoleonic legend in order to describe *The Dynasts* as an "artistic *formation,* definite and explicit, of the reach of man's present consciousness of the world" (p. 187).

12. *The Early Life of Thomas Hardy,* p. 232.

13. Amiya Chakravarty, *The Dynasts and the Post-War Age in Poetry* (Oxford, 1938), p. 22, referred to in Morton D. Zabel, "Hardy in Defense of his Art: The Aesthetic of Incongruity," *The Southern Review,* VI (Summer, 1940), 138-139.

14. Rutland, *Thomas Hardy,* p. 342.

15. Chew, *Thomas Hardy,* p. 135.

16. F. A. Hedgcock, *Thomas Hardy: Penseur et artiste* (Paris, 1911), p. 293.

17. Chew, *Thomas Hardy,* p. 136.

18. Cecil, *Hardy the Novelist,* p. 85. My italics.

19. *Far from the Madding Crowd,* p. 289. My italics.

20. In "The Profitable Reading of Fiction," *The Forum,* V (1888), 57-70, Hardy offers *The Bride of Lammermoor,* the first thirty chapters of *Vanity Fair,* and *Clarissa Harlowe* as examples of formal perfection. He consciously cultivated the "unities" in *The Return of the Native* and in his late play *The Famous Tragedy of the Queen of Cornwall,* of which he wrote: "The unities are strictly preserved, whatever virtue there may be in that. I, myself, am old-fashioned enough to think there *is* a virtue

in it, if it can be done without artificiality. The only other case I remember attempting it in was *The Return of the Native*" (*The Later Years of Thomas Hardy*, p. 235).

21. Lionel Johnson, *The Art of Thomas Hardy* (London, 1895), p. 73.

22. Abercrombie, *Thomas Hardy*, pp. 115, 111.

23. The abstracts prefixed to each book in the serial version are significant. The first book "depicts the scenes which result from *an antagonism between the hopes of four persons*. . . By reason of this strife of wishes, a happy consummation to all concerned is impossible, as matters stand; but *an easing of the situation* is begun by *the inevitable decadence of a too capricious love*, and rumours of a new arrival" (Quoted in Joseph Warren Beach, *The Technique of Thomas Hardy* [Chicago, 1922], p. 94).

24. *Ibid.*, pp. 96, 98, 101, 166-167.

25. *Ibid.*, p. 134.

26. *The Mayor of Casterbridge* is less stylized than *Under the Greenwood Tree*, but even more ordered toward an ending kept constantly in view. *The Return of the Native*, though a great book, alternates between stylization and an attempt to convey the unselective flow of life. *The Well-Beloved* and *The Romantic Adventures of a Milkmaid* are the other markedly stylized books; the former seems to me notably unsuccessful and the latter strikes me as a successfully stylized fairy story in which fairyland and reality interpenetrate in the normal fairy-story manner. Most readers, however, consider it a conventional realistic short novel and as such a grotesquely cheap and implausible one.

27. Albercrombie, *Thomas Hardy*, p. 50; Chew, *Thomas Hardy*, p. 12.

28. Johnson, *The Art of Thomas Hardy*, p. 232.

29. Chew, *Thomas Hardy: Poet and Novelist*, pp. 23, 62.

30. The popular picture of Hardy has become, thanks to criticism, as conventionalized as the popular picture of Pope; it is this fact which makes a rather ungrateful "criticism of criticism" necessary. Once allowance has been made for their premises, many of the books about Hardy can be very useful. Florence Emily Hardy's *The Early Life of Thomas Hardy* (London, 1928) and *The Later Years of Thomas Hardy* (New York, 1930) are readable and human introductions to the biography. Joseph Warren Beach's *The Technique of Thomas Hardy* (Chicago, 1922) and Samuel C. Chew's *Thomas Hardy: Poet and Novelist* (New York, 1928) are useful brief surveys, so long as one makes the necessary reservations. Helen Garwood's *Thomas Hardy: An Illustration of the Philosophy of Schopenhauer* (Philadelphia, 1911) and Ernest Brennecke Jr.'s *Thomas Hardy's Universe: A Study of a Poet's Mind* (New York, 1924), which emphasize the German sources of the "system," should be supplemented by William R. Rutland's survey of the English sources (*Thomas Hardy: A Study of His Writings and Their Background* [Oxford, 1938]) and Harvey Curtis Webster's *On a Darkling Plain* (Chicago, 1947). Mr. Webster's book offers

valuable material on the intellectual trends of Victorian England. Arthur McDowall's *Thomas Hardy: A Critical Study* (London, 1931) and the 1940 Thomas Hardy Centennial Issue of *The Southern Review* (especially the essays by Baker, Davidson, Zabel, and Katherine Anne Porter) seem to me the best critical studies, though there is much to be said for Lascelles Abercrombie's *Thomas Hardy: A Critical Study* (New York, 1912) which combines sensitive analysis with a fine statement of Hardy's general attitude. *The Southern Review* has excellent articles on the poetry. Ruth Firor's *Folkways in Thomas Hardy* (Philadelphia, 1931) is an admirable special study; those who have access to it will find Philip Judson Farley's unpublished dissertation, "Pattern, Structure, and Form in the Novels of Thomas Hardy," (University of California, 1942) a provocative treatment of its subject. For new and general information one may profitably turn to Rutland and to Carl J. Weber's *Hardy of Wessex: His Life and Literary Career* (New York, 1940). Mr. Weber is of course the most devoted of Hardy specialists today. Like many specialists, he has unfortunately succumbed to source hunting and irrelevant annotation. Two amusing examples from Mr. Weber's edition of *An Indiscretion in the Life of an Heiress* (Baltimore, 1935) may serve as a warning to all so tempted. Egbert and Geraldine remain in Egbert's schoolhouse to keep out of the rain—"an echo of the famous rain that influenced the lives of Aeneas and Dido" (p. 45n). A comparison is made between Egbert and Wellington surveying the field of Waterloo—"This reference to the famous battle of 1815 helps to date the action" (p. 54n).

31. *The Early Life of Thomas Hardy,* p. 192.

32. See Albert Feuillerat, *Paul Bourget* (Paris, 1937). See Louis Cazamian, *Le roman et les idées en angleterre: L'influence de la science 1860-90* (Strasbourg, 1923) for the intellectualist tendencies discernible in minor English novelists.

33. General preface to the Wessex edition of Hardy's works.

34. *The Early Life of Thomas Hardy,* p. 151.

35. *Ibid.,* p. 163.

36. Entry in diary for March 4, 1886: "Novel-writing as an art cannot go backward. Having reached the analytic stage it must transcend it by going still further in the same direction. Why not by rendering as visible essences, spectres, etc. the abstract thoughts of the analytic school? . . . The human race to be shown as one great network or tissue which quivers in every part when one point is shaken, like a spider's web if touched. Abstract realisms to be in the form of Spirits, Spectral figures, etc." (*The Early Life of Thomas Hardy,* p. 232).

37. *The Woodlanders,* p. 6.

38. I use the dating of the novels worked out by Weber in his *Hardy of Wessex,* p. 182.

39. *The Later Years of Thomas Hardy,* pp. 93-94.

40. Arthur Symons, *A Study of Thomas Hardy* (London, 1927), p. 9.

41. *The Later Years of Thomas Hardy,* p. 30. "You see, Thomas always thinks every maid is a Tess!" the first Mrs. Hardy complained impatiently to Henry W. Nevinson (Nevinson, *Thomas Hardy* [London, 1941], p. 15).

42. *The Early Life of Thomas Hardy,* p. 216.

43. Letter to Rider Haggard, in *The Later Years of Thomas Hardy,* p. 95.

44. See J. O. Bailey's excellent article, "Hardy's 'Mephistophelian Visitants,'" *PMLA,* LXI (December, 1946), 1146-84. Professor Bailey does not include Manston in his list, but does include Mrs. Endorfield, Sergeant Troy, Diggory Venn, Farfrae, and Newson. If not satanic, Manston is at least a highly mysterious Byronic hero.

45. "For South Wessex, the year formed in many ways an extraordinary chronological frontier or transit-line, at which there occurred what one might call a precipice in time. As in a geological 'fault,' we had presented to us a sudden bringing of ancient and modern into absolute contact, such as probably in no other single year since the Conquest was ever witnessed in this part of the country" ("The Fiddler of the Reels," *Life's Little Ironies,* p. 152).

46. "On the Western Circuit," *Life's Little Ironies,* p. 79.

47. *The Woodlanders,* p. 222.

48. Especially in *A Pair of Blue Eyes, The Hand of Ethelberta,* and *The Well-Beloved.*

49. "The Marchioness of Stonehenge," *A Group of Noble Dames.*

50. "The great condition of idealisation in love was present here, that of an association in which, through difference in rank, the petty human elements that enter so largely into life are kept entirely out of sight." (*An Indiscretion in the Life of an Heiress,* ed. by Carl J. Weber [Baltimore, 1935], p. 42).

51. *The Hand of Ethelberta,* p. 185.

52. *The Later Years of Thomas Hardy,* p. 42.

53. In 1890, Captain O'Shea sued his wife for divorce on the grounds of adultery with Parnell.

54. *Tess of the D'Urbervilles,* p. 327.

55. *The Early Life of Thomas Hardy,* p. 289.

56. *Ibid.*, pp. 203-204.

57. In *The Return of the Native, Two on a Tower, The Woodlanders,* and *Jude the Obscure.* The moral is pointed much more sharply in various short stories. See "For Conscience' Sake," "The Melancholy Hussar of the German Legion," and "Alicia's Diary" in *Life's Little Ironies;* "Enter a Dragoon" and "The Waiting Supper" in *A Changed Man;* "Interlopers at the Knap" in *Wessex Tales.*

58. This has been best stated by Morton D. Zabel. The "radical" quality of Hardy's art "derives from the conjunction, in his temperament, of con-

formist and eccentric tendencies; in his humanism, of stoic acquiescence and moral protest; in his understanding of human character, of a kinship with local, rudimentary, and naturally stable types ('humours' developing toward symbolism) and a sympathy with the gifted, rebellious, or destructive aberrations from the human norm" ("Hardy in Defense of his Art," *The Southern Review,* VI [Summer, 1940], 125-126). Do we not find the same conjunction in Conrad—whose reasoned sympathy, however, was with the stable and whose kinship was with the eccentric?

59. *The Woodlanders,* p. 196.

60. "How severe the tragedy, or how merciful the mitigation of it, depends in part upon whether impulse be given free rein or held in check" (Chew, *Thomas Hardy,* p. 139).

61. *The Later Years of Thomas Hardy,* p. 23.

62. "For Conscience' Sake," *Life's Little Ironies,* p. 37.

63. Preface, *Far from the Madding Crowd.* My italics.

64. Weber, "Hardy's Lost Novel," *An Indiscretion in the Life of an Heiress,* p. 14. It seems much more reasonable to suppose that Hardy wrote of the same tranter and even perhaps of the same country scenes in *Under the Greenwood Tree,* but assumed an entirely new tone and attitude. A novelist may use a single idea or experience not only twice but many times—and each time quite differently. The reappearance of a subject does not justify the assumption that part of a lost manuscript has been used.

65. *The Early Life of Thomas Hardy,* p. 131.

66. See Walter de la Mare's "Some Women Novelists of the 'Seventies," in *The Eighteen-Seventies,* ed. by Harley Granville-Barker (New York, 1929), pp. 45-80.

67. Gissing wrote to Hardy: "In literature my interests begin and end; I hope to make my life and all its acquirements subservient to my ideal of artistic creation" (*The Early Life of Thomas Hardy,* p. 239).

68. *Ibid.,* p. 291.

69. *Desperate Remedies,* pp. 90-101. See pp. 103-105 for a discussion of this attachment.

70. Weber, *Hardy of Wessex,* p. 62. The "humanitarians" were Americans.

71. *The Athenaeum,* May 29, 1886, cited in Rutland, *Thomas Hardy,* p. 199.

72. *Figures of Transition* (New York, 1939), p. 124.

73. *The Early Life of Thomas Hardy,* p. 131.

74. *Ibid.,* p. 300.

75. *Ibid.,* p. 32.

76. *The Later Years of Thomas Hardy,* p. 260.

77. One easily visualizes him at Lady Portsmouth's house party in 1885, a party "mostly composed of 'better halves' " (*The Early Life of Thomas Hardy,* p. 222).

78. *Ibid.*, p. 292.

79. *Ibid.*, p. 42.

80. *The Later Years of Thomas Hardy,* pp. 179, 185, 263.

81. d'Exideuil, *The Human Pair in the Work of Thomas Hardy,* p. xix.

82. *Thomas Hardy,* p. 138.

83. *The Later Years of Thomas Hardy,* p. 168; *The Early Life of Thomas Hardy,* p. 243.

84. Chapters 36-40.

85. *A Laodicean,* p. 137.

86. Dare is, as Somerset says, "a being of no age, no nationality, and no behavior" (p. 81). Dare describes himself as "a citizen of the world" (p. 161) who comes from "going to and fro in the earth, and walking up and down in it, as Satan said to his Maker" (p. 180). Captain De Stancy is right in calling him "quite a Mephistopheles" (p. 188), for he is "graceless" (p. 203)—a lover of gambling who shows a preternatural insight into motives. Even after he has been humanized he recovers his diabolic knowledge at least once: when he recounts Abner Power's obscure history in intimate detail. J. O. Bailey was disturbed by the failure of Dare's name to suggest Mephistopheles (as do the names of some of the other visitants). But does it not suggest *daredevil?* For Professor Bailey's illuminating discussion of Dare see, "Hardy's 'Mephistophelian Visitants,'" *PMLA,* LXI (December, 1946), 1156-60.

87. For instance: "Throughout a long space he had perservered in his system of rigidly incarcerating within himself all instincts towards the opposite sex, with a resolution that would not have disgraced a much stronger man. . . And thus, though he had irretrievably exhausted the relish of society, of ambition, of action, and of his profession, the love-force that he had kept immured alive was still a reproducible thing. . . His teetotalism had, with the lapse of years, unconsciously become the outward and visible sign to himself of his secret vows; and a return to its opposite, however mildly done, signified with ceremonious distinctness the formal acceptance of delectations long forsworn" *(A Laodicean,* pp. 203-204).

88. Cecil, *Hardy the Novelist,* p. 161.

89. "The laboured resistance which Lady Constantine's judgment had offered to her rebellious affection ere she learnt that she was a widow, now passed into a bashfulness that rendered her almost as unstable of mood as before. But she was one of that mettle—fervid, cordial, and spontaneous—who had not the heart to spoil a passion; and her affairs having gone to rack and ruin by no fault of her own she was left to a painfully narrowed existence which lent even something of rationality to her attachment" (*Two on a Tower,* p. 105). This is the first of many such passages. Not the fact that it is abstract summary, but the commonplaceness of the abstract summary, makes it objectionable.

90. Every novelist has experienced this. He visualizes clearly a grand culminating scene several hundred pages perhaps (several months or years of actual writing) in advance. Through the long exploratory (imaginative) approach to this scene, his mind naturally forsees and ponders it. But when the time finally comes to write his crucial chapter, he has lived with it too long. Either he visualizes it in such great detail that nothing remains for the imagination to work on, or his feelings about the scene have been exhausted long since, or he finds his technical equipment inadequate for the conveyance of so much now exact knowledge. It would be interesting to know how many novelists write such scenes first and then return to the exploratory chapters; that is, write their books backward.

91. "Then Henchard, scarcely believing the evidence of his senses, rose from his seat, amazed at what he had done. It had been the impulse of a moment. The regard he had lately acquired for Elizabeth, the new-sprung hope of his loneliness that she would be to him a daughter of whom he could feel as proud as of the actual daughter she still believed herself to be, had been stimulated by the unexpected coming of Newson to a greedy exclusiveness in relation to her; so that the sudden prospect of her loss had caused him to speak mad lies like a child, in pure mockery of consequences" (*The Mayor of Casterbridge,* p. 355).

92. No novelists show more minute care for diagrammatic construction, time sequence, and topographical exactitude than those who publish from three to twelve detective novels a year.

93. *The Later Years of Thomas Hardy,* pp. 79-80.

94. *Ibid.,* p. 85.

95. *Far from the Madding Crowd,* p. 220.

96. *Ibid.,* pp. 102, 150, 219.

97. *The Later Years of Thomas Hardy,* p. 42.

98. The best definition of the distinction between the moral and the didactic is to be found in the Foreword to Yvor Winters' *In Defense of Reason* (New York, 1947).

99. *The Early Life of Thomas Hardy,* p. 213.

100. *Jude the Obscure (*Modern Library edition), p. 418. My italics. See also *Tess of the D'Urbervilles,* p. 44.

101. *The Hand of Ethelberta,* p. 336.

102. *The Woodlanders,* p. 21. In the Wessex edition "lonely hour before day" replaces "antelucan hour." The dead clause "looked at in a certain way" and the comma after "hemispheres" are omitted.

103. "I should have added that *The Well-Beloved* is a fanciful exhibition of the artistic nature, and has, I think, some little foundation in fact" (*The Later Years of Thomas Hardy,* p. 61).

104. *The Well-Beloved,* pp. 156-157.

105. The second Mrs. Hardy, usually a woman of good judgment, found that *The Well-Beloved* anticipated Proust and introduced into

modern fiction "the subjective theory of love" (*The Later Years of Thomas Hardy*, p. 60).

106. *The Return of the Native*, p. 247.

107. The earlier revisions from serial to book versions were also concerned with phrasing, but most often with restoring objectionable scenes.

108. *The Early Life of Thomas Hardy*, p. 218.

109. "Afterwards," *Moments of Vision*.

110. See Zabel in *The Southern Review*, VI (Summer, 1940), 133.

111. *The Later Years of Thomas Hardy*, p. 262.

112. *A Pair of Blue Eyes*, p. 41.

113. *The Return of the Native*, pp. 14-15.

114. *Ibid.*, pp. 78, 56.

115. *Far from the Madding Crowd*, pp. 164-165; *Under the Greenwood Tree*, p. 3; *Far from the Madding Crowd*, p. 290; *The Return of the Native*, pp. 440-441; *The Woodlanders*, pp. 215, 22.

116. Weber, *Hardy of Wessex*, pp. 182-183.

117. *Tess of the D'Urbervilles*, pp. 117-118.

118. *The Early Life of Thomas Hardy*, p. 193.

119. *Ibid.*, p. 299.

120. *Ibid.*, p. 198.

121. "The Marchioness of Stonehenge," *A Group of Noble Dames*.

122. *The Mayor of Casterbridge*, p. 358. My italics.

123. "The Winters and the Palmlays," *Life's Little Ironies*.

124. "A Tragedy of Two Ambitions," *Life's Little Ironies;* "A Mere Interlude," *A Changed Man;* "Netty Sargent's Copyhold," *Life's Little Ironies;* "The Withered Arm," *Wessex Tales;* "What the Shepherd Saw," *A Changed Man*.

125. "The Duchess of Hamptonshire," *A Group of Noble Dames*.

126. *A Pair of Blue Eyes*, pp. 252-253.

127. "The Superstitious Man's Story," *Life's Little Ironies*.

128. Beach, *The Technique of Thomas Hardy*, p. 125.

129. "Hardy's 'Mephistophelian Visitants,'" *PMLA*, LXI (December, 1946), 1146-84.

130. *Ibid.*, p. 1153.

131. Cytherea thinks of him as a "mysterious stranger" (*Desperate Remedies*, p. 158).

132. *Ibid.*, p. 157. My italics.

133. "The Three Strangers," *Wessex Tales*.

134. Johnson, *The Art of Thomas Hardy*, p. 55.

135. *A Laodicean*, p. 240; *The Mayor of Casterbridge*, p. 371.

136. *Desperate Remedies*, pp. 64-87, 87ff.

137. *Ibid.*, pp. 97-98.

138. *Ibid.*, pp. 135-136.

139. "Nausea in such circumstances, like midnight watching, fatigue,

trouble, fright, has this marked effect upon the countenance—that it often brings out strongly the divergences of the individual from the norm of his race, accentuating superficial peculiarities to radical distinctions. Unexpected physiognomies will uncover themselves at these times in well-known faces; the aspect becomes invested with the spectral presence of entombed and forgotten ancestors; and family lineaments of special or exclusive cast, which in ordinary moments are masked by a stereotyped expression and mien, start up with crude insistence to the view" ("For Conscience' Sake," *Life's Little Ironies,* pp. 35-36).

140. *Wessex Tales,* 3rd ed., 1896; transferred to *Life's Little Ironies.*

141. Moore, *Conversations in Ebury Street,* p. 123.

142. *An Indiscretion in the Life of an Heiress; Two on a Tower.*

143. *The Later Years of Thomas Hardy,* p. 42.

144. *Ibid.,* p. 42. In his prefatory note for *Jude* of April 1912, Hardy refers to a German reviewer who described Sue as "the first delineation in fiction of the woman who was coming into notice in her thousands every year—the woman of the faminist movement—the slight, pale 'bachelor' girl—the intellectualized, emancipated bundle of nerves that modern conditions were producing, mainly in cities as yet; who does not recognize the necessity for most of her sex to follow marriage as a profession, and boast themselves a superior people because they are licensed to be loved on the premises."

145. *The Mayor of Casterbridge,* p. 406.

146. *The Early Life of Thomas Hardy,* p. 42.

147. *Two on a Tower,* p. 216.

148. *A Laodicean,* pp. 197-200.

149. *The Well-Beloved,* pp. 138, 136.

150. *Far from the Madding Crowd,* p. 345.

151. *Ibid.,* p. 225.

152. *An Indiscretion in the Life of an Heiress,* pp. 71-72.

153. *The Woodlanders,* pp. 95, 283, 289. My italics.

154. *The Hand of Ethelberta,* p. 373; *The Return of the Native,* pp. 94, 332.

155. As reported by Havelock Ellis in d'Exideuil, *The Human Pair in the Work of Thomas Hardy,* p. xix. "In Clym Yeobright's face could be dimly seen the typical countenance of the future. . . The view of life as a thing to be put up with, replacing that zest for existence which was so intense in early civilizations, must ultimately enter so thoroughly into the constitution of the advanced races that its facial expression will become accepted as a new artistic departure. . . The truth seems to be that a long line of disillusive centuries has permanently displaced the Hellenic idea of life, or whatever it may be called" (*The Return of the Native,* p. 205).

156. *A Pair of Blue Eyes,* p. 382.

157. *Ibid.,* p. 363.

158. *Tess of the D'Urbervilles*, p. 278, 279.
159. *Ibid.*, p. 278. My italics.
160. *The Early Life of Thomas Hardy*, p. 42.
161. *Far from the Madding Crowd*, p. 63.
162. *Ibid.*, pp. 173-174.
163. *The Return of the Native*, pp. 28-29.
164. *Desperate Remedies*, p. 150; *The Mayor of Casterbridge*, p. 102.
165. *Under the Greenwood Tree*, p. 119.
166. *Desperate Remedies*, pp. 58, 251.
167. *Under the Greenwood Tree*, p. 148.
168. *A Pair of Blue Eyes*, p. 66.
169. *Desperate Remedies*, pp. 139-143.
170. *Ibid.*, pp. 408-409.
171. *Under the Greenwood Tree*, p. 244.
172. *Ibid.*, pp. 136-137.
173. *A Pair of Blue Eyes*, p. 73.
174. *Ibid.*, p. 331.
175. *Ibid.*, pp. 131-133.
176. *The Return of the Native*, p. 114.
177. *The Mayor of Casterbridge*, pp. 368, 396, 400.
178. *Ibid.*, pp. 151, 229, 151.
179. *Ibid.*, 99, 281, 275, 332.
180. *Ibid.*, p. 347.
181. *Ibid.*, p. 404.
182. *Lord Jim*, Chapter 33.
183. *Jude the Obscure* (Wessex edition), pp. 393-394.

NOTE

The phrasing in the Harper Thin-Paper Edition of the Hardy novels, used here, and the Macmillan Wessex Edition differs in a number of cases. The differences noted below appear in the quotations presented in the text. Page 23: Wessex Edition (p. 270), *self-mistrust* for *self-abasement*. Page 76, first passage: Wessex Edition (pp. 163-164), *snow white* for *clear white*. Page 80: Wessex Edition (pp. 136-137): *whimsical eye* for *the eye; thus* for *there and thus; homely* for *unstudied; outline* for *outlines*. Page 90: Wessex Edition (pp. 241-242), *their place of death* for *their death*. Page 104: Wessex Edition (pp. 93-94), *with all girls* for *with girls*. Page 126, second passage: Wessex Edition (p. 27), *maphrotight* follows both appearances of *slim-looking*. Page 127, first passage: Wessex Edition (p. 143), *to my thinken* follows *shoulders*. Page 128: Wessex Edition (p. 93), *hold his tongue very clever* for *keep a very clever silence; running round* for *running*.

INDEX OF TITLES AND CHARACTERS

References are given to pages where works are mentioned by title; for further discussion see names of characters. Characters are indexed under the name by which they are more commonly known: some are under first names and others under last names. Abbreviations used are: *Life's Little Ironies (LLI), Wessex Tales (WT), A Group of Noble Dames (GND), A Changed Man (CM).*

New Directions Paperbooks

Prince Ilango Adigal, *Shilappadikaram: The Ankle Bracelet.* NDP162.
Corrado Alvaro, *Revolt in Aspromonte.* NDP119.
Chairil Anwar, *Selected Poems.* WPS2.
Djuna Barnes, *Nightwood.* NDP98.
Charles Baudelaire, *Flowers of Evil.*† NDP71.
Eric Bentley, *Bernard Shaw.* NDP59.
Jorge Luis Borges, *Labyrinths.* NDP186.
Alain Bosquet, *Selected Poems.*† WPS4.
Paul Bowles, *The Sheltering Sky.* NDP158.
Kay Boyle, *Thirty Stories.* NDP62.
Breakthrough to Peace. (Anthology) NDP124.
William Bronk, *The World, the Worldless.* NDP157.
Buddha, *The Dhammapada.* (Babbitt translation) NDP160.
Louis-Ferdinand Céline, *Journey to the End of the Night.* NDP84.
Bankim-chandra Chatterjee, *Krishnakanta's Will.* NDP120.
Michal Choromanski, *Jealousy and Medicine.* NDP165.
Maurice Collis, *The Land of the Great Image.* NDP76.
Marco Polo. NDP93.
Contemporary German Poetry.† (Anthology) NDP148.
Gregory Corso, *Happy Birthday of Death.* NDP86.
Long Live Man. NDP127.
There Is Still Time. NDP190.
David Daiches, *Virginia Woolf.* (Revised) NDP96.
Russell Edson, *The Very Thing That Happens.* NDP137.
William Empson, *Some Versions of Pastoral.* NDP92.
Lawrence Ferlinghetti, *A Coney Island of the Mind.* NDP74.
Her. NDP88.
Routines. NDP187.
*Starting from San Francisco.** Gift Edition. NDP169.
Unfair Arguments with Existence. NDP143.
Ronald Firbank, *Two Novels.* NDP128.
Dudley Fitts, *Poems from the Greek Anthology.* NDP60.
F. Scott Fitzgerald, *The Crack-up.* NDP54.
Gustave Flaubert, *Sentimental Education.* NDP63.
Andre Gide, *Dostoevsky.* NDP100.
Goethe, *Faust,* Part I. (MacIntyre translation) NDP70.
Albert J. Guerard, *Thomas Hardy.* NDP185.
James B. Hall, *Us He Devours.* NDP156.
Henry Hatfield, *Goethe.* NDP136.
Thomas Mann. (Revised Edition) NDP101.

John Hawkes, *The Cannibal.* NDP123.
The Lime Twig. NDP95.
Second Skin. NDP146.
Hermann Hesse, *Siddhartha.* NDP65.
Edwin Honig, *García Lorca.* (Revised) NDP102.
Ann Hutchinson, *Labanotation.* NDP104.
Christopher Isherwood, *The Berlin Stories.* NDP134.
Henry James, *Stories of Artists and Writers.* NDP57.
Alfred Jarry, *Ubu Roi.* NDP105.
James Joyce, *Stephen Hero.* NDP133.
Franz Kafka, *Amerika.* NDP117.
Hugh Kenner, *Wyndham Lewis.* NDP167.
de Laclos, *Dangerous Acquaintances.* NDP61.
P. Lal, translator, *Great Sanskrit Plays.* NDP142.
Tommaso Landolfi, *Gogol's Wife and Other Stories.* NDP155.
Denise Levertov, *O Taste and See.* NDP149.
The Jacob's Ladder. NDP112.
Harry Levin, *James Joyce.* NDP87.
García Lorca, *Selected Poems.*† NDP114.
Three Tragedies. NDP52.
Carson McCullers, *The Member of the Wedding.* (Playscript) NDP153.
Thomas Merton, *Bread in the Wilderness.* NDP91.
Clement of Alexandria. Gift Edition. NDP173.
Emblems of a Season of Fury. NDP140.
*Original Child Bomb.** Gift Edition. NDP174.
Selected Poems. NDP85.
Henry Miller, *Big Sur & Oranges of Hieronymus Bosch.* NDP161.
The Colossus of Maroussi. NDP75.
The Cosmological Eye. NDP109.
Henry Miller on Writing. NDP151.
Remember to Remember. NDP111.
*The Smile at the Foot of the Ladder.** Gift Edition. NDP176.
Sunday After the War. NDP110.
The Time of the Assassins. NDP115.
The Wisdom of the Heart. NDP94.
Vladimir Nabokov, *Nikolai Gogol.* NDP78.
A New Directions Reader. (Anthology) NDP135.
New Directions 17. (Anthology) NDP103.
New Directions 18. (Anthology) NDP163.
Frederick Nicklaus, *The Man Who Bit the Sun.* NDP182.
George Oppen, *The Materials.* NDP122.
Boris Pasternak, *Safe Conduct.* NDP77.
Kenneth Patchen, *Because It Is.* NDP83.
The Journal of Albion Moonlight. NDP99.
Selected Poems. NDP160.

Octavio Paz, *Sun Stone.*† (Rukeyser translation) WPS1.
Ezra Pound, *ABC of Reading.* NDP89.
Classic Noh Theatre of Japan. NDP79.
The Confucian Odes. NDP81.
Confucius to Cummings. (Anthology) NDP126.
Love Poems of Ancient Egypt. Gift Edition. NDP178.
Selected Poems. NDP66.
Translations.† (Enlarged Edition) NDP145.
Philip Rahv, *Image and Idea.* NDP67.
Kenneth Rexroth, *Assays.* NDP113.
Bird in the Bush. NDP80.
The Homestead Called Damascus. WPS3
Natural Numbers. (Selected Poems) NDP141.
100 Poems from the Japanese.† NDP147.
Charles Reznikoff, *By the Waters of Manhattan.* NDP121.
Arthur Rimbaud, *Illuminations.*† NDP56.
Season in Hell & Drunken Boat.† NDP97.
Muriel Rukeyser, *Selected Poems.* NDP150.
San Francisco Review Annual No. 1. NDP138.
Jean-Paul Sartre, *Nausea.* NDP82.
Stevie Smith, *Selected Poems.* NDP159.
Stendhal, *Lucien Leuwen.*
Book I: *The Green Huntsman.* NDP107.
Book II: *The Telegraph.* NDP108.
Dylan Thomas, *Adventures in the Skin Trade.* NDP183.
A Child's Christmas in Wales. Gift Edition. NDP181.
Portrait of the Artist as a Young Dog. NDP51.
Quite Early One Morning. NDP90.
Under Milk Wood. NDP73.
Norman Thomas, *Ask at the Unicorn.* NDP129.
Lionel Trilling, *E. M. Forster.* NDP189.
Paul Valéry, *Selected Writings.* NDP184.
Nathanael West, *Miss Lonelyhearts & Day of the Locust.* NDP125.
Tennessee Williams, *In the Winter of Cities.* NDP154.
William Carlos Williams. *In the American Grain.* NDP53.
The Farmers' Daughters. NDP106.
Paterson. Complete. NDP152.
Pictures from Brueghel. (Pulitzer Prize) NDP118.
Selected Poems. NDP131.
Curtis Zahn, *American Contemporary.* NDP139.

* Paperbound over boards. † Bilingual.

Complete descriptive catalog available free on request from New Directions, 333 Sixth Ave., New York 14